HARPER LEE
AND ME

HARPER LEE
AND ME

David Dessauer

XULON PRESS

Mill City Press, Inc.
2301 Lucien Way #415
Maitland, FL 32751
407.339.4217
www.millcitypress.net

Scripture quotations taken from the New King James Version
(NKJV). Copyright © 1982 by Thomas Nelson, Inc. Used by
permission. All rights reserved.

Printed in the United States of America

Paperback ISBN-13: 978-1-6628-0634-6
eBook ISBN-13: 978-1-6628-0635-3

Dedicated to my Brothers, Danny and Mark,
who believed in me even when I sure as hell didn't.

CONTENTS

INTRODUCTION

This will be a bold attempt to do several things at once, first, unlock the secret to Nelle Harper Lee's sepulcher of silence surrounding *To Kill a Mockingbird (TKAM)* second, to swan-dive into all the metaphors, allegories and connections within it unlocking her secret sources of inspiration, and lastly, plead the case and show by a preponderance of evidence that Truman Capote could not have written it.

TKAM is a masterpiece and work of utter genius. But why does Lee not discuss it? What is the reason that keeps her silence so profound and enduring? Her final interview is in 1963 and she dies in 2016, so for over fifty-three years she will not talk about it. Even though her wit and vivacity are well known to her friends and relatives. When she is given well-deserved awards, she demands the organization promise not to ask questions or make her address the adoring crowd. In the 1963 interview she casually mentions that she is more of a *"rewriter than a writer"*.[1] This is essentially the clue as to how she wrote it and a possible explanation of why she will not talk about it at all. Every great work of art, literature and even science has some source of inspiration. And the key to creativity is the ability to hide your sources, so says Albert Einstein. Ben Franklin said that three people can keep a secret if two of them are dead. Lee knew how to keep all her secrets. She is inspired by many sources and my goal is to shed light on these sources and inform the reader that she is doing exactly as she said, *rewriting* some of *TKAM*. She is using resources that have been either overlooked, under-utilized or just plain missed. The main reason being that the story is so good and fascinating that there is no reason to check anywhere else to see if there are any connections. But the connections are there, some are so well hidden it took almost sixty years for them to be unearthed. Others are metaphorical/allegorical and a little abstract, still others are plain bizarre. I hope to demonstrate just how they all come together to understand the beautiful tapestry it is, why unraveling this tapestry Lee could not do, and that Truman Capote could not have written *TKAM*. There is a story within the story of *To Kill a Mockingbird* and after much research and thought couple with plenty of pain and anxiety it can now be told.

Let's start with an easy one. I used her real first name for a reason. She is named after her maternal grandmother Ellen but of course backwards.[2] This will be a theme in some of the metaphors I believe to have found, they will simply be backwards. And she hates being called Nel-*ly* so much that in some *Rammer Jammer (RJ)* mastheads she is recorded as *Nell* not *Nelle*. And they get her name backwards in *RJ 22.2 page 3* as *Nelle Lee Harper*. Some of the action will be a backwards rendering of the source material. If the source or inspiration is a girl then in *TKAM* it will be a boy, if a young person, then Lee writes an older person into the scene. If something is numbered one through twelve then she will write it starting with the twelfth on down to the first, and so forth. This will be a theme throughout the book. Action and speech may be the opposite of a story or picture that is the source of within *TKAM*, just as her name is backwards of Ellen. But this is not the bizarre part.

To me the crazy part is why she includes something like the two thousand-year-old Rosetta Stone in the year of grace 1935 in Maycomb, Alabama. Mr. Avery gets in the act and tells us how the Rosetta Stone predicts inclement weather if kids misbehave. This is certainly not true; however, it should not be considered a lie in a work of fiction. But it is also not funny, so it is not a joke. So, what is it and why is it there? It is a **riddle**, and readers should be asking themselves, "What the Sam Hill is this Rosetta Stone doing here?" Because the Rosetta Stone did solve the riddle of ancient Egyptian hieroglyphics. In fact, the Rosetta Stone is mentioned *twice* within *three* pages. But it took many years and much hard work to come up with the answer to the hieroglyphics. Nelle Lee is possibly laying down a marker to indicate that there are maybe *two* or *three* secrets, storylines or read-between-the-lines cryptic metaphors within her book that need to be deciphered. I hope that it does not take as long as two thousand years to decode. I might not be there for the book signing.

Do not think me nuts because the number of times the Rosetta Stone is mentioned and within the number of pages has significance. The numbers in *TKAM* themselves have alternate meanings and/or foreshadowing of the action and events. Years and dates themselves can foreshadow, have significance or just be an inside joke. Lee's wry wit is on display within the number of chapters. And thanks to the University of Alabama (*Roll Tide*), the *Rammer Jammers* are all online. *I will take Rammer Jammers for $1000, Alex. "This is the number of volumes the Rammer Jammer appeared in." "What is thirty-one?" Correct for $1000 and you are back in the black.* This corresponds to the number of chapters in *TKAM* **thirty-one**. I have found that this is an under-utilized avenue for discovering where Lee receives her creativity. Every biography I have every read gives short shrift to the *Rammer Jammer*. They simply note that she was a contributor in volume twenty-one and editor in volume twenty-two. She wrote a couple of good pieces and a parody of the famous *Yes, Virginia, There Is a Santa Claus* editorial from the *New York Sun* in 1897. But to my knowledge no one has looked at the *RJ's* in depth until now. I looked at all of them all 187 and over 4600 pages and found it a vast wealth of originality and inventiveness, commensurate with the imaginativeness of the writers including Nelle Lee. And Lee was able to use much of it. For what it is worth here is one of the more direct take offs. And for some reason Lee never mentions her first remuneration for writing. She is rewarded with a box of *LifeSavers* for this joke in *RJ 23.2*, November 1947. *One Methodist preacher, speaking to another Methodist preacher about a third said, "I don't wish to call anyone bad names, but when he goes home tonight, I hope his mother runs out from under the porch and bites him."*[3] This joke is not mentioned in any other publication or book concerning Harper Lee. The reason seems simple, after volume 22, her name is not on the masthead as editor or contributor, nor is her name a byline for any article, so there is no reason to include it in

Are you
Maeb eht no*

You are, if you get tongue-tied when you meet a cute cookie! Or worse yet, if you stoop to "weather talk!" *Get on the beam* right, fellow! Start off from third base! Offer that choice bit of calico a yummy Life Saver. She'll be keen on them (and you).

✳ "On the beam" backwards

WINT O GREEN
LIFE SAVERS   5¢

P. S. *Just in case this friendship ripens—Life Savers keep your (and her) breath kissably fresh!*

Each Month a box of Life Savers is given to the person contributing the best joke of the month. This month's winner is NELLE LEE, University, Ala.

One Methodist preacher, speaking to another Methodist preacher about a third, said, "I don't wish to call anyone bad names, but when he goes home tonight, I hope his mother runs out from under the porch and bites him."

19

researching Harper Lee. I found it as I had no idea which volume she worked on. I only knew it was in the 1940's and started to dig. Here is that joke as presented in *RJ 23.2*. Lee is calling the third minister a son of a bitch, but only if you think about it and make the connection that his mother is the dog under the porch. Otherwise it has no meaning and would never had been LifeSaver-worthy. I purposefully included the cartoon of the girl and her embarrassed beau.

Here is why from *TKAM; There was an odd thing about Miss Maudie—on her porch she was too far away for us to see her features clearly, but we could always catch her mood by the way she stood. She was now standing arms akimbo, her shoulders drooping a little, her head cocked to one side, her glasses winking in the sunlight. We knew she wore a grin of utmost wickedness.*[4] It is Lee herself with the wink and grin as she helps herself to this picture to describe Miss Maudie and winking at the reader, grinning at her own ironic wickedness. Lee is injecting herself in her own book. Comparing this picture to Miss Maudie does not seem a stretch to me, there are so many similarities to relate to. Particularly as it is within spitting distance of her SOB joke and includes a backwards phrase like her first name.

But there is a relation to many other books, stories and pictures. Now comes the bizarre part. There are thirty-one chapters in the Old Testament Book of *Proverbs*. Right after the description of Miss Maudie developed from the picture above, a self-righteous woman on the way to the trial of Tom Robinson blasts out from *Ecclesiastes 6:4*, "*He that cometh in vanity departeth in darkness.*"[5] Miss Maudie retorts from *Proverbs 15:13*, "*A merry heart maketh a cheerful countenance.*"[6] *Ecclesiastes* follows *Proverbs* in the Old Testament.

So, we have thirty-one chapters of *TKAM, Rammer Jammers* and *Proverbs*. But it does not end there. *Proverbs* contains much wisdom, so much so that Lee seems to include her reason for silence within a specific one. Harper Lee lets us know from Scout's own mouth in chapter four. Here the kids are playing to a radio show *with a **specific number**, One Man's Family, Chapter XXV, Book II.*[7] *Rammer Jammer 28.7, page 13* references the show, *One Man's Family*, all of which had a book and chapter just like all the *Rammer Jammer's* volume and number. The chapter and book seemed odd to me. What could be so special about an exact show that the full cataloging of the chapter and book needed to be written? How could that possibly add anything to the texture of *TKAM*? If fact it **does not** add anything to *TKAM*. But it does add something that supports my research and reasoning. It just took a little time and not a little faith to see what Lee is doing and where she is going with these number references. Lee is actually referring to ***Proverbs 25.2, It is the glory of God to conceal things, but the glory of kings to search things out**. **This is her secret theme throughout the book**. I decided to search the things out that Nelle Harper Lee desires to conceal. I believe she took her secrets to the grave because of this passage. Miss Maudie's own words urged me on, *"Don't worry about me, Jean Louise Finch. There are ways of doing things you don't know about."*[8] I think Lee is injecting herself in the book with these words. And why not, it is her first book, she has no idea of the impact it will have. Or that it is also her last book. Once hooked on this hunt these words were a throwing down of the gauntlet to uncover her secrets by me. And, in finding them gave me a far greater appreciation of this book. I would go as far as to say that the book she writes is even better than the book one reads. But this is only possible if you make the kind of connections and follow the clues to the all other references she is metaphorically, symbolically and allegorically alluding to. It is more than reading between the lines you must do as Alice does and go through the looking glass and see what is on the other side of the words, phrases, dates and even the numbers themselves that are within *To Kill a Mockingbird*. And constantly ask *why* something does or does not happen, *why* something is there or not there. If you do your appreciation of this book will grow and grow.

In conclusion, if Truman Capote had written it then I believe that there is no way he could have kept the same Sphinx-like silence that Lee does about all the interesting goings on within the words themselves. As Wayne Flynt writes in *Mockingbird Songs My Friendship with Harper Lee,... if Truman had written any part of TKAM, he would not have only hinted the allegations at cocktail parties, he would have flashed the news in neon on Times Square, especially in his hazy twilight years.*[9] Plus, I doubt that he had access to the *Rammer Jammers* otherwise he would have spilled the beans long ago. Because I will show that those are the source of far more than Miss Maudie's moods. *TKAM* may even be a sort of rebirth of the *Rammer Jammer* as they were discontinued in a few months before Christmas in 1956. Christmas of 1956 was a life-changer for Lee. And given his lifestyle I cannot fathom him knowing *Proverbs* has thirty-one chapters and would consciously use that same number for the chapters in *TKAM.* I hope this ends that ugly rumor for good.

CHAPTER 1

In the book, *The Mockingbird Next Door: Life With Harper Lee,* by Marja Mills, Nelle Harper Lee is quoted as saying, *"I wish I'd never written the damn thing."*[10] I can see why. *To Kill A Mockingbird* has plagued me too. I have been on a hunt for many years to find all the meanings, metaphors and sources for the words within. If my theory is correct, and I can only call it a theory as I cannot prove beyond all doubt that what I am saying is true, then I have found the extraordinary source material and meaning to the words themselves and the inside story of how she wrote *To Kill a Mockingbird, and why she refused to discuss it.* You can read the book and understand the words. What I have found is that there are more implications and meaning to the words themselves in the story. You cannot just look at the words, you have read past them, through them, turn them around, see them in the light of a genius. See them for what they are. They are words of poetry, artistry, riddles, jokes, clues, metaphors, allegories, parables, stories out of place and references out of time. It is no wonder she could not write another book. No one could replicate *TKAM*, not even Nelle Harper Lee. Any other book would have been a moon-cast shadow. And she was too much Harper Lee to be satisfied with anything less. There is only one tomb of Tutankhamun and I have found the literary equivalent within the words written by Nelle Harper Lee.

Yes, what I am saying may offend some, confuse others and mystify many. But what I desire is to enlighten. To get at the heart, soul and mind of Lee as she writes this book as an unknown, sometimes suffering and often lonely writer. Writing is so difficult, the blank page stares back at you and often laughs, knowing it is far stronger than you. It can do nothing and win, the writer must pour forth the words in order to not fail. It is the desire to avoid failure that is the key. Success is too strong a word to use when writing. Success is fleeting, like the baby that grows much too fast into an adult. Through an adolescence that almost makes the parent as crazy as the teenager. I see my children grow and I want to cry like a baby for the past when they needed and longed just for me. To wonder where the past went and how the time seems to slip past at whirlwind speed. That is what writing is like. It lays there like a lover that is unsatisfied and longing for more, demanding more and willing to leave at any moment to find someone, or something that satisfies. Leaving you humiliated. Writing is like a drug that cannot be legalized, only momentarily sated. Lee knew this all too well. Hell, she even threw the entire book out the window at one time in utter frustration. There is a single word for this, but my brother, Mark, made me take it out; defenestration is that word. But her publisher made her go out in the snow and pick it all up. I know I would not have had the courage to do the same.

There is the rub, Lee had the courage to finish this book. A book that is more hidden, uncovered and secret than anything else. Why? This is the word that must be used in reading *TKAM*. Why something happens or *does not happen*. Why is a certain word used or *not used*. Who is really speaking and what are they really saying. Why is the key to this book, you cannot use pick and shovel to understand all the metaphors, allegories, symbolism and connections. It would be much easier if you could. You must ask **why**. And you must think. Thinking about things that seem similar or at least have some correlation. You must look at it from a distance to see what is really going on. There is a painting named, *Gala Contemplating the Mediterranean Sea which at Twenty Meters Becomes the Portrait of Abraham Lincoln-Homage to Rothko*, by Salvador Dalí. If you never see it from twenty meters you cannot see Lincoln. Fortunately, Dalí clued us in on the secret. Harper Lee does no such thing. *TKAM* is the same, it must be seen from different perspectives to understand the secrets. The connections that must be made are like one of my favorite movies, *In the Heat of the Night*. In it, Sidney Poitier solves the murder by making a connection and seeing and hearing what is really going on and what is really being said. In short, a rich guy is murdered and robbed. Our hero is caught up in it. But the key to understanding who the murderer is, is in a scene that only seems to have nothing to do with the murder. A man comes into the police station with his underage sister who is pregnant. She obviously lies about who the father is. And Sidney sees a motive for murdering someone with money, the real father needs money for an illegal and expensive abortion. He does not see an ignorant, poor, pregnant girl, he sees something no one else does, motive for murder in a scene that on the surface has nothing to do with the actual murder. He does a deep think that connects two events that on the surface have no correlation. *TKAM* is the same as the painting and the movie. More is going on under the scene than is on the surface. Harper Lee's words are the tip of the iceberg, but whereas the iceberg is ninety percent under water, her story is often over one hundred percent unseen. This is what I want to reveal.

Let's start at the beginning. Jean Louise Finch or *Scout* is our narrator. She is a child of either six or eight. But there is no reason given for this unusual nickname. To this day I hear the name Harper given to boys as well as girls, but I never hear the name *Scout* for any child. So where would this nickname come from? Why would anyone nickname a child, boy or girl this? Nelle Harper Lee must have some furtive reason for *Scout* but never reveals it. At the time she is writing the only other known Scout is Tonto's horse in *The Lone Ranger*. I wonder if that concerned her, well, probably not. But Scout's name is so unusual I think I found it in equally extraordinary way. Suffice it to say not only am I tormented like Lee with this book I suffer from depression. At my lowest point I turned to the Bible for some solace and hope. As a Catholic I head to chapel and open our Catholic Bible. There are books we have that other denominations do not. They are called *Apocrypha*. *Sirach* is one that is not in most Protestant Bibles and probably the reason Lee uses this book to name Scout. She knows right away that she will need to hide her sources and starts here. Again I want to reiterate that what I am putting down you need not pick up, if I sound cock-sure of something that is not provable I want the reader to know that I know this, I just get tired of putting in qualifiers like maybe, seems like or possibly. It is also a little boring to write that way, so please excuse me now and later if something is theorized without said qualifier. I open the Bible to this passage, *Sirach 14:21-27, The Happiness in Seeking Wisdom; Happy is the person who mediates on Wisdom and reason intelligently, who reflects in his heart on her ways and ponders her secrets, pursuing her like a* **scout***, and lying in wait on her paths, who peers through her windows and listens at her doors; who camps near her house and fastens his tent peg to her walls; who pitches his tent near her, and so occupies an excellent lodging place; who places his children under her shelter, and lodges under her boughs; who is sheltered by her from heat and dwells in the midst of her glory.* Jean Louise Finch's nickname leaps out at me, infecting my brain like a virus. Rereading *TKAM* dawns on me that all these words of *Sirach* are paraphrased in *TKAM* one way or another. The most glaring is the fact that Jem is in a *tent-like arrangement* [11] to keep the covers off at the very end. It just seems so out of place. The doctor could have used a splint, a sling or even a cast, but Lee puts Jem in something using *tent* to fulfill *Sirach*. She had to stick in *tent* somewhere and could only come up with it here at the end. I believe Scout is named after this passage. And she uses a book of the Bible that is not well known in order to hide her source. Because what is well hidden within *TKAM* is why she will not talk about it. Her sources may be revealed and as Albert Einstein said, the secret to creativity is the ability to conceal your sources. Had she been able to talk about it she may not have later in life wished that she had never written it. Because the source material is so well hidden or overlooked and used so blatantly that she could, in some small-minded circles, considered to have plagiarized. I would never use such a despicable word, I just want others to know that she is inspired by other works like most great artists, scientists and writers. But she shall never reveal this, only leave clues to her methods, metaphors and connections throughout *TKAM*. Her inability to talk about it leaves her lonely and she seems to even have a drinking problem later in life. She seems so rightfully proud of *TKAM* she cannot separate herself from it. If *TKAM* loses face or prestige in some circles she may have felt too much guilt. I think Nelle Harper Lee embodies Oscar Wilde's bon mot truth that; *There are only two tragedies in life: one is not getting what one wants, and the other is getting it.* Sadly, Harper Lee may have been a sufferer of both types of tragedy.

About the time I start my research and writing, her draft book is discovered. *Go Set a Watchman (GSAW)* is published in 2015 and well received as it should. Lee makes it no secret that the title is from *Isaiah 21.6*, which is in every Bible. But in the Catholic Bible, *Isaiah* follows *Sirach*. A pattern starts to emerge. One thing follows another. One source is connected to another, sometimes it is in the Bible, but other times it is something far too mundane to even consider. Because the numbers, be they on coins, concerning dates, ages, times or any reference to a numeral has significance. Sometimes they need to be added up and or subtracted using the algebra Scout and Jem are to later learn to see the light. Even the number of chapters and parts is a big deal to me. Because it was the other clue to unmasking Lee's mysteries. There are two parts and thirty-one chapters. Most would ho-hum this little fact, not so your fearless author. I gather the courage to call the University of Alabama to see if she might have taken a Bible as Literature or some such class. They refuse to tell me anything concerning her classes, but gladly inform me that all the *Rammer Jammers* are now online. I thank them and start to look the *Rammer Jammer* over.

Back in the day, every college worth its mortar boards would have a humor magazine. Think of the *Harvard Lampoon* on every campus. There was *The MIT Voo-Doo, The Wabash Caveman, The Dartmouth Jackolantern* and *The*

University of Minnesota Ski-U-Mah (don't ask) to name a few. All using humor to get through tough classes and prepare for the future. Nelle Harper Lee was a contributor in volume twenty-one and editor in volume twenty-two of the *Rammer Jammer*. All had a volume and number assigned to them. This has significance so write it down. I have already introduced *Proverbs 25.2, It is the glory of God to conceal things, but the glory of kings to search things out.* And the fact that there are thirty-one chapters in *Proverbs, TKAM* and *Rammer Jammers.* All these and much more will be a source for *TKAM.* Let us start at the very beginning of *TKAM.* Jem is in love with football and football has always been a huge part of the University of Alabama experience, **Roll Tide.** In fact, *Rammer Jammer* was the football cheer it goes:

Hey, Auburn, Hey Auburn, Hey Auburn, We just beat the hell outta' you! Rammer Jammer, Yellow Hammer, Give 'em hell, Alabama.

"Denny was never like this"

Jem is of course injured at the end of *TKAM,* but Lee starts with Jem's love of football and this description of his injury. I may have found where she got the idea for this and the reason for any boy to love football. There appears to be a corresponding cartoon in two different *RJ's, 16.3* and *21.4*[12] with quite the reason to love football.

When he was nearly thirteen, my brother Jem got his arm badly broken at the elbow. When it healed, and Jem's fear of never being able to play football were assuaged, he was seldom self-conscious about his injury. His left arm was somewhat shorter than his right; when he stood or walked, the back of his hand was at right angles to his body, his thumb parallel to his thigh.[13] Note how our nearly thirteen, number **twelve**, football player hands bear a striking resemblance to the injuries that Jem sustained in the attack, left thumb is parallel to his thigh, hand opposite is at a right angle and a hen's tooth longer. Nelle Lee's name is in the latter *Rammer Jammer 21.4* as contributor or *Scribbling Ram,* she therefore has reason, however slight, to assume someone, somewhere, some-how at some time may still have this *RJ 21.4* and make this link. If someone does than maybe it all becomes known, maybe all her secrects are revealed. I think that she even wanted someone other than Gregory Peck for the roll of Atticus for the simple reason that he graced the pages of *Rammer Jammer 25.5, page 28* in a cigarette ad. And just like our *Proverbs 25.2* clue from chapter four, Lee may have injected a clue leading to this particular *Rammer Jammer 25.5.* As Dill wins five dollars in a beautiful child contest, then goes to the movies twenty times and leaves the next day on the five o'clock bus. Since the twenty and the first five are on the same page we add them for twenty-five and the other five is in the next chapter we have, of course, **twenty-five five**. Because we have another contestant for an important character to be gleaned from the pages of the same *Vol. 25, Number 5 Rammer Jammer.*[14]

"Boo."

He is none other than one of the most enigmatic and mysterious characters in all of modern American Literature. Arthur "Boo" Radley can be seen in this cartoon of the drooling, cat and squirrel eating big dog with scars across his face if you use the MRI of the mind, read the caption, ***"Boo"***, note the dad's eyes popping out and realize that Harper Lee does have secrets that she needs to keep. *Jem gave a reasonable description of Boo: Boo was about six-and-a-half-feet tall, judging from his tracks; he dined on raw squirrels and any cats he could catch, that's why his hands were bloodstained - if you* *ate an animal raw, you could never wash the blood off. There was a long jagged scar that ran across his face; what teeth he had were yellow and rotten; his eyes popped, and he drooled most of the time. "Let's try to make him come out," said Dill. "I'd like to see what he looks like." Jem said if Dill wanted to get himself killed, all he had to do was go up and knock on the front door.*[15]

But I do not think that she leaves the *RJ's* alone for long as she may have used this cartoon from one of the last ones *RJ 31.6*[16] to complete the picture of the six foot-six inch Boo Radley with bloodstained hands and skull that accosts Miss Stephanie Crawford, plus *RJ 28.6 page 5* has an equally bloodthirsty creature that also fits this description. *Miss Stephanie Crawford said she woke up in the middle of the night one time and saw him looking straight through the window at her…said his head was like a skull lookin' at her.*[17] Lee likes to think outside the lunchbox and spread the wealth when it comes to utilizing the

Rammer Jammer. Because 25.2 not only points to *Proverbs,* but also *Rammer Jammer 25.2.* The pictures, cartoons and jokes within this *RJ* alone could account for her silence.

The next chapter will more fully expound on the use of pictures and images from *RJ 25.2* and cement the use of *Proverbs 25.2* theme within the secret *TKAM*.

CHAPTER 2

L et's start with an in-depth look at the *Rammer Jammer 25.2*. Just as *TKAM* starts with a reference to the Battle of Hasting in 1066, *Being Southerners, it was a source of shame to some members of the family that we had no recorded ancestors on either side of the Battle of Hasting.*[18] *RJ 25.2* also mentions the winner of this battle, William the Conqueror is also known as William the Bastard King of England noted in a story on page 5 of *RJ 25.2*.

Lee seems to lead right off the bat with this particular *Rammer Jammer* and never lets it go. She will start and end with stuff from this one, and use others, but *RJ 25.2* is her baby. Jem is color blind and so is someone on the Pep Squad on page 5 of *RJ 25.2*.

Arthur "Boo" Radley may be chained to the bed as a form of punishment, we have another author chained up in *RJ 25.2*.[19] And this may have been the way Lee felt in writing. Boo is supposed to be up the chimney in *TKAM* and Scout is scared, but I doubt if she is as scared as our woefull pledges in this picture, one has stuffed himself up the chimney right next to Boo Radley.[20]

*Jem hissed, "Scout, how's he gonna know what we're doin'? Besides, I don't think he's still there. He died years ago and they **stuffed him up the chimney**." Dill said, "Jem, you and me can play and Scout can watch if she's **scared**."*[21] If Scout is insulted by being called "Miss Priss"[22] than look no further than *RJ 19.8 page 20* for another useage of the term "Miss Priss". And if Scout gives Jem a picture of Dixie Howell to assuage his grief than look in *RJ 18.3 page 45* to see Mr. Howell again.

The pageant *Ad Astra Per Aspera* is a crucial part of the book and in my theory it too has a double meaning that will be explained later. But just for now, know that the first part *Ad Astra* is also in our star *Rammer Jammer 25.2 page 14.*

X Billups is a minor character in chapter sixteen, and there is a small ad in *RJ 25.2* for a Billups gas station with the planes looking like an X.[23] Lee is ever the good editor and wants the advertisers to be patronized. Had they bought a bigger ad we may have been reading about Arthur "Boo" *Billups* and X **Radley.** More about X later as he is actually a very important person.

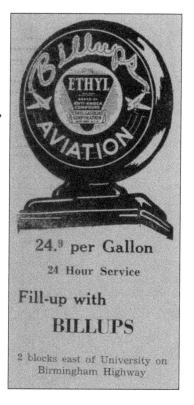

24.⁹ per Gallon
24 Hour Service
Fill-up with
BILLUPS
2 blocks east of University on Birmingham Highway

As is Dill. He is described, *Dill was a curiosity. He wore blue linen shorts that buttoned to his shirt, his hair was snow white and stuck to his head like duckfluff; ...he habitually pulled at a cowlick in the center of his forehead.*[24] So here he is in all his *Rammer Jammer* glory from *RJ 25.2* note the white hair, cowlick, buttons attached to shirt and the age old curiosity of boy meets girl. Dill is a mash-up of these two boys, I believe.[25]

"Lay off, Penrod. She's nothing but a damn barfly."

But the most difficult one to discern is next. Both Mr. Radley and Boo are, I think, taken from these pictures in *RJ 25.2*. Please read the descriptions and take a real long look at all the pictures from *RJ 25.2* below.[26] And recall that it is in chapter four that the number 25.2 is introduced and our professor is on page four. *He was a thin leathery man with colorless eyes, so colorless they did not reflect light. His cheekbones were sharp and his mouth was wide, with a thin upper lip and a full lower lip. Miss Stephanie Crawford said he was so upright he took the word of God as his only law, and we believed her, because Mr. Radley's posture was ramrod straight.*[27]

Our professor is sitting on something pretty ramrod straight and has full lower and thinner upper lips, colorless eyes, wide mouth, and sharp cheekbones. And from the passage below he has a torn shirt, jutting chin, sickly white hands and face, hands on slate, thumb in belt, hollow cheeks, thin, feathery hair and an image blurred by the pipe smoke.

Lee is describing Boo Radley in Chapter 29. *He was still leaning against the wall. He had been leaning against the wall when I came into the room, his arms folded across his chest. As I pointed he brought his arms down and pressed the palms of his hands against the wall. They were white hands, sickly white hands that had never seen the sun, so white they stood out garishly against the dull cream wall in the dim light of Jem's room. I looked from his hands to his sand-stained khaki pants; my eyes traveled up his thin frame to his torn denim shirt. His face was as white as his hands, but for a shadow on his jutting chin. His cheeks were thin to hollowness; his mouth was wide; there were shallow, almost delicate indentations at his temples, and his gray eyes were so colorless I thought he was blind. His hair was dead and thin, almost feathery on the top of his head. When I pointed to him his palms slipped slightly, leaving greasy sweat streaks on the wall, and he hooked his thumb in his belt. A strange spasm shook him, as if his fingernails scrape slate,*

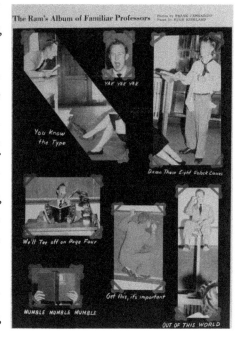

but as I gazed at him in wonder the tension slowly drained from his face. His lips parted into a timid smile, and our neighbor's images blurred with my sudden tears.[28]

It would not surprise me that Lee is again referring to herself when she mentions tears, as they could be tears of her own laughter as her ingenious and original sense of humor gets the better of her and she utilizes so many aspects of these pictures she cannot help but laugh at herself. Because if you think about it sand and khaki are the same color, so sand cannot stain khaki. Our professor himself tells us how important it is, right next to his image being blurred by pipe smoke and sitting on a ramrod straight pole, or thin frame, with his thumb in his belt that goes up to his torn shirt.

Chapter five Dill sees an elephant so he must have noticed the elephant cartoon in *RJ 25.2, page 21*. Miss Maudie also seems in on the secrets and states, *Miss Maudie shook her head... "The things that happen to people we never really know. What happens in houses behind closed doors, what secrets-"*[29]

These words can be interpreted different ways, but I will assert that it is Lee again referring to herself and the secret story within a story of *TKAM*. If you only read the words, and

never ask *why,* the true meaning can slip and slide right past you.

Scout also wants to get in on the act as she describes Stephanie Crawford, *He looks like Miss Stephanie Crawford with her hands on her hips,' I said. 'Fat in the middle and little-bitty arms.*[30] Our coed in *RJ 25.2*[31] is not so amused by this description, however on target.

If Aunt Alexandria wears a corset then she must have read our *RJ 25.2 page 9* first, it has a story of a woman wearing a corset. And if the kids play strip poker than all they have to do is go to *RJ 31.2 page 14* and see another poor soul that played strip poker all night. As well as *RJ 25.5 page 25* has a joke about strip poker. Jem Finch must read to Mrs. Dubose, just so a reader is needed in an article in *RJ 20.2 page 12* that said reader must enter a house with a Mrs. Finch in it.

Jem loses his pants, but he is not the only one. Our law student in *RJ 25.2*[32] seems to be as cheeky as Lee. Who was herself a law student at one time. So she knows that keeping quiet about the possible use of this material is critical. As it might lead to some trouble even if it is in the public eye. Because in one

"Another damn Law student"

of the following issues, *RJ 25.5*, where I believe she uses the image of a dog to flesh out Boo, and where Gregory Peck is in an ad, is actually called the *Swipped Edition* as the staff decide to use other college humor magazines material to meet their own deadline. They had a bit of spring fever and decided to swipe an issue for the *Rammer Jammer Volume 25, number 5* instead of producing their own. *Rammer Jammer 25.5 on page 5* even has its own motto, stolen from the *Dartmouth Jackolantern*: *Plagiarism Is An Art; Practice It Carefully.* As we progress, keep in mind *Proverbs 25.2, It is the glory of God to conceal things, but the glory of kings to search things out.* Small wonder she wrote that number in Roman numerals, just one smaller layer of deception to conceal and help her abide by *Proverbs 25.2.*

I think that the vast majority of readers along with me would never even think to accuse Harper Lee of plagiarism, but who knows what she herself thought. She refused to talk about it, her silence was deafening.

CHAPTER 3

Harper Lee's mastery with words is only exceeded by her innate and unique ability to hide her allusions, metaphors and foreshadowing. She can even double down by obscuring her intended reference. Lee foreshadows events and develops characters without writing a single word. You just have to know where to look up her actual image and what she is really saying using *Proverbs 25.2* and its hiding theme seems to confirm this. And to prove same, let's look at some of the conversations, testimony and features of Tom Robinson's "trial".

The most memorable to me is the date of the alleged rape itself. It is stated **six** times between chapters seventeen to nineteen as November Twenty-First. Maybe being one letter away from sex is another little Lee joke. But she again utilizes the wisdom inherent in the Bible and we read in *Proverbs 11:21, Though the wicked join hand in hand; the children of the righteous shall be delivered.* She foreshadows the rescue of Jem and Scout without writing one word. But we know she has a wicked and sinful sense of humor and enjoys exhibiting it. So

I decide to see if the date itself has any significance, and you have to hand it to her, because it is pretty ballsy and off-the-wall to juxtapose a rape with none other than the *Feast Day of The Presentation of the Blessed Virgin Mary* in the Roman Catholic calender, also November Twenty-First.

But the kids must first be attacked before they can be saved, so where is this? Again pretty good stuff as Calpurnia enters the courtroom looking for Jem and Scout. None other than Mr. Underwood prophetically states that they come in at exactly one-eighteen p.m. Mr. Ewell would be upset to know that he is not going to survive as we turn to *Proverbs 1:17-18, For in vain is the net baited while the bird is looking on. Yet they lie in wait to kill themselves! And set an ambush for their own lives!* Underwood adding the p.m. seems to indicate not only *Proverbs* but *Psalms* is utilitized. Read *Psalm 118:20-22, This is the gate of the Lord; the righteous shall enter through it. I thank you that you have answered me and have become my salvation. The stone that the builders have rejected has become the chief cornerstone.* This may be the verse Lee is alluding to and getting back at all the rejections she receives prior to *TKAM.* As well as thanking the Lord for the opportunity to write at all. It seems a bit of an understatement to call *TKAM* a cornerstone of American Literature. Underwood is the brand of typewriter that Lee uses to write *TKAM,* we will see more of Mr. Braxton Bragg Underwood later, thanks to *Proverbs 25.2.*

Tom rejects Mayella Ewell and will die for it. She asks him onto the property to bust up a chiffarobe and of course our *RJ 17.4 page 16* has the very same hussy of a chiffarobe used in a sexual connotation. Tom is the only one on the stand other than Heck Tate during the trial that you can believe. He states that Mayella takes one year to save seven nickels to clear out the other children so she can seduce Tom. In fact, Lee doubles down on the deception and has Tom echoing Mayella in court concealing **seven** with "*seb'm*"; '*...took me a slap year to save **seb'm nickels**, but I done it.*³³ Proverbs 7:5, *that they may keep you from the loose woman, from the seductress with her smooth words. Proverbs 7* reads in full:

My child, keep my words and store up my commandments with you; keep my commandments and live, keep my teachings as the apple of your eye; bind them on your fingers, write them on the tablet of your heart. Say to wisdom **"you are my sister,"** *and call insight your intimate friend,* **that they may keep you from the loose woman, from the seductress with her smooth words.** *For at the window of my house I look out through my lattice, and I saw among the simple ones, I observe among the youths,* **a young man without sense,** *passing along the street near her corner,* **taking the road to her house** *in the twilight, in the evening, at the time of night and darkness. Then a woman comes toward him, decked out like a prostitute, wily of heart.* **She is loud and wayward;** *her feet do not stay at home; now in the street now in the squares, and at every corner she lies in wait.* **She seizes and kisses him, and with an imprudent face she**

says to him: "I had to offer sacrifices and today *I have paid my vows; so now I have come out to meet you, to seek you eagerly, and I have found you! I have decked my couch with coverings colored spreads with Egyptian linen; I have perfumed my bed with myrrh, aloes, and cinnamon.* **Come, let us take our fill of love until morning; let us delight ourselves in love.** *For my husband is not at home; he had gone on a long journey. He took a bag of money with him; he will not come home until full moon" With much seductive speech she persuades him; with her smooth talk she compels him. Right away he follows her, and goes like an ox to the slaughter, or bounds like a stag toward the trap until an arrow pieces its entrails.* **He is like a bird rushing into a snare, not knowing that it will cost him his life.** *And now, my children, listen to me, and be attentive to the words of my mouth. Do not let your hearts turn aside to her ways; do not stray into her paths. For many are those she has laid low, and numerous are her victims. Her house is the way to hell going down to the chambers of death.*

Lee is doing the same thing Hugo does in *Les Misérables*; however she uses *Proverbs 7* instead of *Psalms 109*. The connections to *Les Misérables* will be explored more in Chapter Seven. Jean Valjean's 109 francs alludes to *Psalm 109* and is a microcosm of *Les Misérables*, just so *Proverbs 7* is a brief synopsis of *TKAM*, with Mayella as the seductress and Tom is the dead bird.

Mayella also has geraniums. Seems a bit odd to me to designate that flower, until I happened upon a certain *RJ*

29.2 page 25 with an article about a wolfess (seductress) that needs three things, men, romance and geraniums and if she cannot have the first two she better darn well have the third. And it hits me like a ton of bricks. Lee ever the good editor is doing what every editor worth their geraniums is doing. Lee is saying patronize our advertisers, florist whose ad was and still is; *Say it With Flowers.* There are many such ads in the *RJ*, such as one from 9.7, page 20 *Cannas, azaleas,* and *Snow-on-the-Mountain* all play a roll in the secrets of *TKAM*. Harper Lee is metaphorically using the secrets of flowers by what they represent, certain qualities and attributes, even by how they are spelled. She really and truly is saying it with flowers. Such as our geraniums, our wolfess may need them because, well, they ejaculate their seeds in order to disperse them, so there, who needs men anyway.

Let's start with azaleas, since they are also mentioned in *Les Misérables.* Azaleas are so toxic that according to *Wikipedia: Azaleas and rhododendrons were once so infamous for their toxicity that to receive a bouquet of their flowers in a black vase was a well-known death threat.* At the end of *Les Misérables,* Part Five, Book Nine, Chapter Five, Jean Valjean states, *"I'm going to die in a little while."*[34] A handful of paragraphs prior, Cosette states, *"…The azaleas are coming along nicely."*[35] Azaleas are associated with death and to get a vase of them was the sleep with the fishes threat. Because that is exactly the story of the Old Testament Lee is referring to in chapter ten with the rabid dog Atticus kills. Which also has the most important line of all, *"That's why it is a sin to kill a mockingbird."*[36] Rabies is also known as hydrophobia, or fear of water, and the most feared water of all times was the flood of Noah. Chapter ten's secret is its parallels and connections with the flood of Noah from *Genesis 6-9.*

Miss Maudie gets the ball rolling speaking of Atticus, *"There's life in him yet." "…he can make somebodies will so airtight can't anybody meddle with it."*[37] God **wills** Noah to make the ark, *Genesis 6:14, Make yourself an Ark of Cypress wood; make rooms in the ark and cover it inside and out with pitch.* The pitch makes it water-tight if not airtight. Miss Maudie starts our flower show, *"Now keep out of the way of the carpenters. You'd better go home. I'll be in my azaleas and can't watch you. Plank might hit you."*[38] Death noted by the azaleas and the carpenters making something with wood parallel the flood of death and the building of the Ark. Scout is skeptical that there even could be a rabid dog in February, the flood starts in the second month, *Genesis 7:11, In the six hundred year of Noah's life, in the **second month**, on the seventeenth day of the month on that day all the great fountains of the great deep burst forth, and the windows of the heavens were opened.* The last time the word *yawl* is used when Zeebo takes care of the dead dog. *"Don't yawl come over here for a while,"*[39] he called. *Yawl* has an alternative meaning that seems to bolster my idea and dovetails with the *Proverbs 25.2* theme of concealing things, seeing as Lee could have easily spelled it *ya'll*. **Yawl** is also a boat, definitively; *a two masted fore-and-aft-rigged* *sailboat with the mizzenmast.* This word *yawl* or *ya'll* should be in *TKAM* hundreds of times but only three times does Lee use it. She seems to emphasis the importance of this word by its absence, just like the absence of the word Christian, only used three times as well, in the New Testament.

As Atticus starts to shoot the dog Scout states,...*I thought he moved like an **underwater** swimmer: time had slowed to a nauseating crawl.*[40] Miss Maudie sings Atticus's praises, "*Forgot to tell you the other day that besides playing the Jew's Harp, Atticus was the deadest shot in Maycomb county in his time*" ... "*Why, down at the Landing when he was coming up, if he shot **fifteen** times and hit fourteen doves he'd complain about wasting ammunition.*"[41] Genesis, that nice Jewish book describes the flood in deadly terms, *Genesis 7:20-21, the waters swelled above the mountains covering them **fifteen** cubits deep. All flesh died that moved on the earth, birds, domestic animals, wild animals, all swarming creatures that swarm the earth, and all human beings. Genesis 8:8, Then he sent out the dove from him, to see if the waters had subsided from the face of the ground.*

"O. K., Goldstein, here's your harp."
—We is such obliged to you all, Tiger

Genesis 8:11, and the dove came back to him in the evening, and there in its beak was a freshly plucked olive leaf; so Noah knew that the waters had subsided from the earth. But the dove does not return in *Genesis 8:12, Then he waited another seven days, and sent out the dove; and it did not return to him anymore.* Like the fifteenth dove that Atticus did not kill, but its landing is not recorded. We do have record of Atticus's Jew's harp in *Rammer Jammer 8.5.*[42]

The *Chesterfield* word game contorts and tortures *Tabor* into *Robot*. Following the rules of this *Rammer Jammer 25.2 page 21,* word game one can easily twist and shout *Jew's Harp* into *Jew's Ark,* by dropping the *H* and replacing the *p* with a *k.* This is far less work than the *Tabor/Robot* metamorphosis above and reminds us of *Proverbs 25.2.* Noah needs an **ark for water**, but Lee can only get in an *arc of water* in chapter six. *Mr. Avery sat on the porch every night until nine o'clock and sneezed. One evening we were privileged to witness a performance by him which seemed to have been his positively last, for he never did it again so long as we watched. ... a closer inspection revealed an **arc of water** descending from the leaves and splashing in a yellow circle of the street light, some ten feet from source to earth, it seemed to us.*[43] We will see Mr. Avery again in another *Proverbs 25.2* context.

Let's continue to say it with flowers in the Old Testament. *TKAM* Chapter **eight** notes snow, and surprise, exactly *eight* inches of snow falls in Alabama, recorded in *RJ 23.4 page 5.* Scout knows nothing of snow, the Rosetta Stone and Miss

Maudie's fire are all prominent. And Lee does of nice job of starting off with a flower that is the Swiss Army Knife of metaphors. *Old Mrs. Radley died that winter, but her death caused hardly a ripple-the neighborhood seldom saw her, except when she watered her cannas.*[44] There are three reasons that Mrs. Radley has cannas. First, they are spelled almost like Canaan, the promised land that is pledged to Abraham by God that Moses led the Hebrews to in *Exodus* after the Passover, next, they rhyme with manna, the food God provides to the Jews in the wilderness on the way to said promised land of Canaan, lastly, most mind-boggling of all, cannas are **edible**, just like the aforementioned manna. Nelle Harper Lee's *Proverbs 25.2* secret here is the fact that she writes about both the Passover and *Exodus* in chapter eight. Since we cannot have Passover without someone dying then *Old Mrs. Radley* is chosen to suffer the death reserved for the firstborn of Israel. The very young of Egypt die in the first Passover, so Lee writes that an old person passes away, the reverse of firstborn, recall our Nelle/Ellen association.

This is the reason why Rosetta Stone is conspicuous. ...*it was written on the Rosetta Stone that when children disobeyed their parents, smoked cigarettes and made war on each other, the seasons would change.*[45] The Rosetta Stone is three languages in one story that allowed the ancient Egyptian hieroglyphics to be translated. Matched with the three reasons for cannas seems to be the kind of tie that Lee would make that she would also want to be kept a secret. The Rosetta Stone is a three in one message and cannas are a three in one metaphor. And a way of getting in the word *Egypt* without writing it in specifically.

Passover is always started with the youngest asking why this night is different. *"Ask him,"* Jem whispered. *"You ask him you're the oldest." "That's why you oughta ask him." "Atticus,"* I said, *"did you see Mr. Arthur?"*[46] Mr. Arthur "Boo" Radley being the subject of the kid's desire to see and make come out, just as the Jews want to come out of the slavery of Egypt in *Exodus*. And *Exodus 16* has the miracle of manna and of course *TKAM* has **sixteen** prominently displayed as the cold temperature that leads to the snow. Just as Scout is mystified by snow, neither do the Hebrews know what manna is. *Exodus 16:14-15, When the layer of dew lifted, there on the surface of the wilderness was a fine flaky substance, as fine as the frost on the ground. When the Israelites saw it, they said to one another: "What is it?" For they did not know what it was.* The kids gather the snow and dirt to make a snowman. The snowman is called the Absolute Morphodite symbolizing the Pharaoh of Egypt. Lee even includes the worms in the gathering of the snow and dirt. *Jem ran to the back yard, produced the garden hoe and began digging quickly behind the woodpile, placing any worms he found to one side.*[47] Wouldn't you know it, worms are associated with manna as well, *Exodus 16:20, But they did not listen to Moses; some left a part of it until morning, and it bred worms and became foul.*

Miss Maudie's house fire represents the pillar of fire that helped the escaping Hebrews and killed Egyptians, and a fire is in a prominent story in *RJ 25.4 page 8. Exodus 14:24, At the morning watch the Lord in the pillar of fire and cloud looked down upon the Egyptian army and threw them into panic.* Panic ensues in *TKAM* as the fire trucks are slow in arriving. *We saw why. The old fire truck, killed by the cold, was being pushed from town by a crowd of men. When the men attached the hose to the hydrant, the hose burst and water shot up, tinkling down on the pavement. "Oh-h Lord, Jem…" Jem put his arm around me. "Hush, Scout," he said. "It ain't time to worry yet. I'll let you know when."*[48] *Exodus 14:26, Then the Lord said to Moses, "Stretch out your hand over the sea so that the water may come back upon the Egyptians, upon their chariots and chariot drivers."* Miss Maudie is almost delighted by the fire to her house and tends to her charred frozen *azaleas.* And we all know that these flowers are just as deadly as the fire. She understands the symbolism so well she almost tells us so in Harper Lee's voice, *"Don't worry about me, Jean Louise Finch. There are ways of doing things you don't know about."*[49] This is the lead into ending this chapter in almost the same way as Exodus ends. *Miss Maudie stared down at me, her lips moving silently. Suddenly she put her hands to her head and whooped. When we left her she was still chuckling. Jem said he didn't know what was the matter with her-that was just Miss Maudie.*[50] In the Bible, Miriam whoops it up with all the women at the end of *Exodus,* with her hand on a tambourine.

Miss Maudie's hands are on the only instrument available to her, the voice in her head. *Exodus 15:20-21, Then the prophet Miriam, Aaron's sister, took a tambourine in her hand; and all the women went out after her with tambourines and **dancing**. And Miriam sang to them: "Sing to the Lord, for he has triumphed gloriously; horse and rider he has thrown into the sea."* As all the women celebrate, Scout must get in on the act and states, ***By dancing** a little I could feel my feet.*[51]

We can celebrate our next flower and it needs no introduction, just an extensive explanation that will seem almost mystical and supernatural. Because this flower is the Elvis Presley (may he rest in peace), the Mac-Daddy (whatever that means), and the Charlie Brown (I've always liked Charlie Brown) of metaphors, allegories and symbolism. It is a big deal. It is the *Snow-On-The Mountain* Jem receives from Mrs. Dubose. But first a little botany class is in order. Our flower, the *Snow-On the Mountain,* is **toxic**, here is the description from Wikipedia: ***Warning:** Plant parts (fresh or dried) and extracts made from them can be toxic if ingested to both humans and cattle. Ingestion causes inflammation or blistering of the mouth, throat, and esophagus. Contact with plant can cause irritation of skin, eyes, and mucous membranes. Sensitivity to a toxin varies with a person's age, weight, physical condition, and individual susceptibility. **Children are most vulnerable because of their curiosity and small size.** Toxicity can vary in a plant according to season, the plant's different parts, and its stage of growth; and plants can absorb toxic substances, such* as herbicides, pesticides, and pollutants from the water, air, and soil. It is toxic but not fatal, unlike azaleas. The family name is *spurge*. Lee chose this flower very carefully and after much research. Of course, there are other flowers in this family, such as *Scarlet Plume* and *Fire-on-the Mountain* and *Poinsettias*. But for our purposes let's consider only two spurges; *Devil's Backbone* and *Crown-of-Thorns*.

The first is easy, Jem calls Dubose a devil just like our flower. But as soon as given to him from Dubose, Jem is in agony. *Jem opened the box. Inside, surrounded by wads of damp cotton, was a white, waxy perfect camellia. It was a Snow-on-the Mountain. Jem's eyes nearly popped out of his head. "Old hell-devil, old hell-devil!" he screamed, flinging it down. "Why can't she leave me alone?" In a flash Atticus was up and standing over him. Jem buried his face in Atticus's shirt front. "Sh-h," he said. "I think that was her way of telling you everything's all right, Jem, everything's all right…" Jem raised his head. His face was scarlet. Jem picked up the candy box and threw it in the fire. He picked up the camellia, and when I went off to bed I saw him fingering the wide petals.*[52] The second flower is not so simple to understand. To decipher Harper Lee's true intention and *Proverbs 25.2* secret we must dig a little. Since a *Snow-on-the-Mountain* is also a spurge. If my theory holds than it is the *Crown-of-Thorns* that Lee is indicating and alluding to, she uses *Snow-on-the-Mountain* as camouflage. just in her oblique and roundabout way that you must think about. We know that a *Crown-of-Thorns* is a spurge and that it is toxic.

But it is not lethal, this is the key. Jesus Christ is scourged in all four Gospels, but it does not kill him. Lee uses a flower that is a spurge and is toxic but not deadly to refer to Christ's scourging prior to his crucifixion. The closeness of the names, scourge and spurge and what their characteristics and qualities are in and of themselves lead me to this conclusion. Jesus prays to God in the Garden of Gethsemane is the converse or mirror image of Jem's asking the *hell-devil* to leave him alone. *Luke 22:42 "Father if you are willing, remove this cup from me; yet not my will but yours be done."* Atticus comforts Jem just like the angel that strengthened Christ. *Luke 22:43-44, Then an angel from heaven appeared to Him and gave him strength. In His anguish he prayed more earnestly, and sweat became like great drops of blood falling down on the ground.* Jem's face is scarlet, but Atticus's shirt catches the blood that is why Jem's face is in his shirt. Jesus is also given a scarlet robe in in *Matthew 27:28-29, They stripped him and put a scarlet robe on him, and after twisting some thorns into a crown, they put it on his head. They put a reed in his right hand and knelt before him and mocked him, saying, "Hail, King of the Jews!"* Christ is the true mockingbird in *To Kill a Mockingbird*. Jem, Scout and Boo Radley all play a role in representing Him. Jem's role is now known to him as he sees his own scourged, tortured, bloody, dead body in the spurge written as *Snow-on-the-Mountain* but should be read as **Crown-of-Thorns**. But as Scout is not yet nine, she is unaware. This knowledge will later be made known to her; she will have her own Agony in the Garden. If there is any "coming of age" in *TKAM* for Scout it is this awareness of her symbolic crucifixion in the coming Pageant, known as *From the Mud to the Stars. Rammer Jammer volume 22, number 3, page 4,* has something similar, *Mud on the Stars,* and the hell Christ went through and descended into is next to it, Lee is the editor. Transforming and understanding that the Pageant, *Ad Astra Per Aspera* is the Passion of Christ will be the *Proverbs 25.2* secret that Harper Lee can never reveal.

CHAPTER 4

O k, you have turned the page and have accepted my premise to one degree or another that the pageant *Ad Astra Per Aspera* is the **Passion of the Christ**. Because put into context this addresses many questions and interesting occurences that occur constantly in *TKAM*. It also answers some difficult question. Why does it answer such questions? Since it is at the end of *TKAM* then all action prior is before Christ dies on the cross and proves himself the Lamb of God, or in Latin, *Agnus Dei* and is also in Part 3 Book II Chapter VIII, in *Les Misérables*. But Lee gets it in surreptitiously in *TKAM*, *"Agnes, is your father home? Oh God, where is he?"*[53] Later to be made into a play and movie, *Agnes of God* is a play on words that translates the Latin, *Agnus Dei* to *Lamb of God*. Atticus represents God in *TKAM*.

Atticus during the trial calls 1935 a year of *grace*. Interesting word choice, *grace*, but fairly non-descript when Year of our Lord is far more common as that is what A.D. means in Latin, *Anno Domini* or **Year of our Lord**. Atticus cannot say year of our Lord as it has not happened yet. In

TKAM Lee is rewriting the Bible, the Pageant is the Passion of Christ and therefore things associated with our Christian world are simply not in Maycomb county because they have yet to occur. Just as Christ is mocked and laughed at on the cross, so too will Scout as she represents Him and she is ridiculed and jeer at on the stage in the pageant. This furtive secret also seems to shed light on Lee's dogged determination to never speak a word about *TKAM;* if one secret is revealed then all will eventually become uncovered. This also fufills another *Proverb. Proverbs 25.9, Argue your case with your neighbor directly, and do not disclose another's secret.* So why start in the first place, just remain silent and let the words speak for themselves. She has no idea how many *Rammer Jammers* still exist in old files and hidden in nooks and crannies that might be looked at once the book and movie are a smashing success. How long would it take for someone to connect the thirty-one volumes in the *Rammer Jammers* to thirty-one chapters in *TKAM* then one day to thirty-one chapter of *Proverbs*? Actually the answer to that question is about fifty-five years.

Let's start with a tough question first. In Latin, the pageant is called *Ad Astra Per Aspera.* This is a well know phrase from Roman times that translates, *To the stars through hardships.* It is the state motto of Kansas and the first part, *to the stars, Ad Astra* is in noted in *RJ 25.2, page 14.* Of course, this connects to our *Proverbs 25.2, It is the glory of God to conceal things, but the glory of kings to search things out.* But Lee

mistranslates this famous phrase by calling it, *"from the mud to the stars."[54]* Why? The answer is simple, she wants to, plus it connects to *RJ 22.3, page 6, Mud on the Stars* is noted in an article. *Luto* is mud in Latin. Lee must know this as her strength is her research. But someone else is misquoted while speaking an unfamiliar language. And it transpires during the Passion of Christ. The only time in any Gospel that Jesus speaks in another language He is *misinterpreted*, probably by the more rustic types. *Mark 15:33-35, Now when the sixth hour had come, there was darkness over the whole land until the ninth hour. And at the ninth hour Jesus cried out with a loud voice, saying, "Eloi, Eloi, lama sabachthani?" Which is translated, "My God, My God, why have you forsaken me?" Some of those who stood by, when they heard that, said, "Look, He is calling for Elijah!"* Jesus is quoting *Psalms 22.1 a Psalm of David, My God, My God, why have you forsaken me? Why are you so far from helping me from the words of my groaning?* If Jesus can reference a Psalm at death then Lee can no doubt apply a Proverb to her life's work. Lee is following this biblical account but needs to conceal it to continue her *Proverbs 25.2* theme therefore she writes in *TKAM, Mrs. Merriweather, stationed behind her lectern beside the band, said: "Maycomb County Ad Astra Per Aspera." The bass band boomed again, "That means," said Mrs. Merriweather, translating for the rustic elements, "from the mud to the stars." She added, unnecessarily, it seemed to me, "A pageant"[55]* Read *Pageant* as *Passion of Christ.* These two phrases will be interchangeable for the purposes of exploring her silence and understanding the hidden meanings in *TKAM*.

Atticus is nowhere near the pageant and this comports to the Christ's words on the cross as He dies. Atticus represent God the Father so he cannot be at the pageant. In fact, the only time Scout refers to him as Mr. Finch, his most formal title, is as Cecil Jacobs confronts and scares Jem and Scout. Note his initials are C.J. the opposite of J.C for Jesus Christ. *Someone leaped at us. "God almighty!" Jem yelled. A circle of light burst in our faces, and Cecil Jacobs jumped in glee behind it. "Ha-a-a, gotcha!" he shrieked. "Thought you'd be comin along this way!" "What are you doin' way out here by yourself, boy? Ain't you **scared of Boo Radley**?" Cecil had ridden safely to the **auditorium** with his parents, hadn't seen us, then had ventured down this far because he knew good and well we'd be coming along. He thought Mr. Finch'd be with us though.*[56] As a shriek would hurt ears and the lights may be a nod to the betrayal and trial of Christ. *Luke 18:3&10, So Judas brought a detachment of soldiers together with police from the chief priests and the Pharisees, and they came there with lanterns and torches and weapons. Then Simon Peter, who had a sword, drew it, struck the high priest's slave, cut off his right ear. The slaves name was Malchus. John19:8-10, When Pilate heard this statement he was even more afraid. He went back into the **Praetorium**. "Where are you from?" he asked, but Jesus gave no answer. So Pilate said to Him."Do you refuse to speak to me? Do You not know that I have authority to release*

You and authority to crucify You?" The reason Atticus is not at the pageant is because he had been in Montgomery all week. Montgomery being the capital of Alabama is a muted reference to Jerusalem, the capital of Israel and where Jesus must enter His Passion and be crucified. *When Halloween came, I assumed that the whole family would be present to watch me perform, but I was disappointed. Atticus said as tactfully as he could the he just didn't think he could stand a pageant tonight, he was all in. He had been in Montgomery for a week and had come home late that after noon.*[57] Jesus is in Jerusaleum for an entire week, our Holy Week. And Aunt Alexandera cannot go either but gets in our foreshadowing and mimics Christ during His trial. *Aunt Alexandra said she just had to go to bed early, she'd been decorating the stage all after noon and was worn out-she stopped short in the middle of her sentence. She closed her mouth, then opened it to say something,* **but no words came.** *" 'smatter, Aunty?" I asked. "Oh nothing, nothing," she said,* **"somebody just walked over my grave."**[58] Here Lee may have been inspired by *Luke 11:43&44, "Woe to you Pharises! For you love to have the seat of honor in the synagogues and to be greeted with respect in the marketplaces Woe to you! For you are like* **unmarked graves, and people walk over them without realizing it.**" Scout continues; *She put away from her whatever it was that gave her a pinprick of apprehension, and suggested that I give the family a preview in the livingroom. So Jem squeezed me into my costume, stood at the livingroom door, called out "Po-ork," exactly as*

*Mrs. Merriweather would have done, and I marched in. Atticus and Aunt Alexandrea were **delighted**.[59]* Jesus is bound before Pilate just as Scout is squeezed into her costume and speaks no words. Christ has no words for Pilate and Pilate is as amazed just as Atticus and Aunt Alexandrea are delighted. *Mark 15:1-5 As soon as it was morning, the chief priests held a consultation with the elders and scribes and the whole council. They bound Jesus, led him away, and handed him over to Pilate. Pilate asked him, "Are you the King of the Jews?" He answered him, "You say so." The the chief priests accused him of many things. Pilate asked him again, "Have you no answer? See how many charges they bring against you." But Jesus made no further reply, so Pilate was **amazed**.*

Throughout this entire process I would ask questions and the answers seemed to appear out of nowhere. I wondered why there was no cross in Cal's church or in the happy cemetery, why a teacher would not know why Hitler persecuted the Jews. Miss Gates states in chapter 26, *"There are no better people in the world than the Jews, and why Hitler doesn't think so is a mystery to me"* An inquiring soul in the middle of the room said, *"Why don't they like Jews, you reckon, Miss Gates?"* *"**I don't know, Henry**."[60]* It just seemed inconceivable to me that an educated person in Bible Belt 'Bama does not know why Jews are so tormented. Lee makes no secret of it in *Go Set a Watchman,…our Jewish friends… killed Christ*.[61] But in *TKAM*, **Christ has not yet been crucified**, it simply hasn't happened yet. This is why I call the Pageant the Passion of the Christ. Harper Lee is using her literary license to bring the salvation of the world via her beloved Maycomb County, Alabama.

The Romans actually kill Christ but the Jews are forever associated with His death and they say it themselves in *Matthew 27:25, Then the people as a whole answered, "His blood be on us and our children."* This Roman connection may be the reason she references *One Man's Family* in **Roman numerals** as *Chapter XXV, Book II*. It appears to be a logical *Proverbs 25.2* connection. Why else bother with Roman numerals when Scout and the family would have heard it on the radio and rarely if ever read about it in the paper or a magazine. Including Roman numerals further connecting *TKAM* to our most proverbial *Rammer Jammer, Vol. XXV No. 2.*

It also took many years for another aspect of *TKAM* to reveal its secrets. Calpurnia's church has only one picture, Hunt's *Light of the World.* Painted about 1853, Hunt was silent on its symbolism for over 50 years. Not until the early 1900's did he tell us that the picture is a metaphor for opening the mind to Christ, but only from the **inside.** Christ is at the door but there is ***no door handle***, the heart of Christ can only be received from the inside. What is not there is the actual locus of the action and underlying meaning. One must open the door from within to meet and know Christ, just like the Boo Radley game the kids play. They want Boo to come out; Hunt wants Christ to come in, another Nelle/Ellen reversal. *"Let's try to make him come out," said Dill. "I'd like to see what he looks like." Jem said if Dill wanted to get himself killed, all he had to do was go up and knock on the front door.*[62] Just as Christ knocks on the door and will be killed. Hunt is inspired by *Revelation 3:20, Behold I stand at the door and knock; if any man hear my voice, and open the door, I will come in to him and will sup with him, and he with Me.* Lee goes into quite the detail in describing Cal's church and its cemetery in chapter 12, but again no cross in either the happy cemetery or the unceiled church, corresponding to the door lacking a handle in the only picture in the church.

Dill predicts Scout will die in three days in chapter four. Dill will represent the Old Testament in *TKAM*. In chapter four, *"No, I mean I can smell somebody an' tell if they're gonna die. An old lady taught me how." Dill leaned over and sniffed me. "Jean-Louise-Finch, you are going to die in three days"*[63] Just as the Old Testament predicts the New Testament, and the New fulfills the Old; Lee has Scout dying in three days instead of rising as Christ resurrects on the third day. Dill using all of Scout's real first names indicates to me that Dill is referring to the Three in One God or Father, Son, and Holy Spirit. Recall that Nelle Harper Lee's first name is the opposite of her namesake, Ellen. The conversation continues and the first of only three times is the word *yawl* used. *"Yawl hush," growled Jem, "you act like you believe in Hot Steams."*[64] But she gets in another prediction of death by way of mythology. Jean Louise Finch, our Scout, reads so much she is considered a **Bullfinch**, not just a *finch* in Chapter two, "...*Jem says my name's really Jean Louise Bullfinch, that I was swapped when I was born and I'm really a-"*[65] Later in chapter four Jem's death is alluded to, but you have to understand the mythological reference. ...*I played that summer with more anxiety despite Jem's assurances that Boo Radley was dead and nothing would get me, with him and Calpurnia there in the daytime and Atticus home at night. **Jem was a born hero.***[66] Just as Scout's death is foreshadowed by Dill, Jem's death is presaged by calling him **hero** and by the fact that this one sentence is a paragraph all by itself. If you read *Bulfinch Illustrated Mythology* then you will know that *Hero* is a girl and kills herself when she finds out that her lover Leander has died as he tries to swim across the Hellespont to reach her. *But one night a tempest arose and the sea was rough; Leander's strength failed, and he was drowned. The waves bore his body to the European shore, where Hero became aware of his death, and in despair cast herself down from the tower into the sea and perished. ... The story of Leander's swimming the*

Hellespont was looked upon as fabulous, and that the feat considered impossible, until Lord Byron proved its possibility by
performing it himself.[67] Lee even misspells Bulfinch, adding
an additional *"l"* to help hide this allusion. Of course, Nelle
Harper Lee's *Rammer Jammer* cannot be without the story of
Hero and Leander, noted in *RJ 14.3, page 11*.

Calpurnia is prominent throughout *TKAM* and her
name may have similar relevance to the secrets Harper Lee
is hiding as she practically lives with the Finch's. Cal is even
upbraided for it at her church by Lula, described as; *She
was bullet-headed with strange almond-shaped eyes, straight
nose, and an Indian-bow mouth. She seemed seven feet high.
"Yeah, an I reckon you's comp'ny at the Finch house durin' the
week."*[68] Harper Lee may have been inspired by this picture

of a popular cartoon character of the time, *Little
Lulu* to flesh out **Lula.**
This name Lula is also
found in our *Rammer
Jammer 9.6 on page 15.*
Capernaum is where
Jesus lives during His
three-year ministry. *Mark
2.1, When He returned to
Capernaum after some days,
it was reported that he was
at home. Matthew 4:13-16,*

*He left Nazareth and made his home in **Capernaum** by the sea, in the territory of Zebulum and Naphtali, so that what had been spoken through the prophet **Isaiah** might be fulfilled: Land of Zebulum, Land of Naphtali, on the road by the sea, across the Jordan, Galilee of the Gentiles—the people who sat in darkness have seen a great light, and for those who sat in the region and shadow of death light has dawned.* The title, *Go Set a Watchman,* the parent and precursor to *TKAM* is taken from *Isaiah 21.6.* Capernaum and Calpurnia are as close to each other as needed for my *Proverbs 25.2* theme here in the hidden *TKAM.*

Certainly, you need not believe that she uses parts of *Little Lulu* for **Lula,** but it seems that both have an Indian-bow mouth, bullet head and almond eyes. Since being seven feet tall is the exact opposite of little this corresponds to the reversal aspect of her modus operandi. I think I have established a pattern for Harper Lee in that she will use some aspects of an article or picture, not others, and adds her own embellishments that adhere to the *TKAM* storyline.

This is the main reason that Truman Capote her childhood friend and collaborator on his book, *In Cold Blood,* could not have written *TKAM.* He could not have kept his bloody mouth shut about all these connections, influences and metaphors. It would be hard to fathom that Capote had access to the *Rammer Jammer* magazines and you cannot tell me that he is reading the Bible and knows that *Proverbs* has thirty-one chapters, so that *TKAM* will also need that number of chapters; or that in *Les Misérables,* Jean Valjean is as good with a gun as Atticus, does not shot birds, braves a fire to help someone, and buys Cosette on Christmas day. Image the fun Truman Capote might have had exposing *The 12 Days of Christmas* hidden within *TKAM.* Small wonder Lee could be so silent about her incredible work, she has to be given the secrets within and the importance of *Proverbs 25.2, It is the glory of God to conceal things, but the glory of kings to search things out.*

CHAPTER 5

Tom Robinson is scared and will die and he knows it. His trial is coming but first he must face the mob. Just as Christ faced a hatefilled mob on Good Friday. Thankfully, my brother, Danny, pointed out that *1 Samuel* also has thirty-one chapters in the Old Testament. This contains the famous scene where David kills Goliath and the Philistine army runs away in panic. How does this relate to *TKAM*? Well, I'll tell you. It is interesting and illuminating all at the same time. Harper Lee at her best in hiding her references to the Bible. David is the second most named man in the Bible and Mr. Underwood shall represent him. First, Harper Lee is using an Underwood brand typewriter and sees this name every day. David is the writer of many of the psalms in the *Book of Psalms,* just as Mr. Underwood is sole (that word again, *sole/soul*) owner of the local paper *The Maycomb Tribune* and writes all the articles. Braxton Bragg is Underwood's first and middle names and this is also the name of a famous Confederate general, and that same name is in an article noted in *RJ 13.2, page 8* with Lee used as his last name, *Braxton Bragg Lee*. Again the *Rammer Jammer* having what *TKAM* includes. Harper Lee could have used any name at all for Mr. Underwood, but purposefully used a name that corresponds to a *Rammer Jammer* reference. David, in the Bible, was famous for his military exploits, as well as his writing the psalms and they even sing about them in *1 Samuel 18:6-7, As they were coming home, when David returned from killing Philistines, the women came out of all the towns of Israel, singing and dancing, to meet King Saul, with tambourines, with songs of joy, and with musical instruments. And the women sang to one another as they made merry, "Saul has killed his thousands, and David his ten thousands."*

Mr. Underwood is further described, *His days were spent at his linotype, where he refreshed himself occasionally from an ever-present gallon jug of cherry wine. He rarely gathered news; people brought it to him. It was said that he made up every edition of The Maycomb Tribune out of his own head and wrote it down on the linotype. This was believable.*[69] Underwood also lives above the Tribune and can see the jail that Tom is in from his window. The mob is planning on lynching Tom and Atticus must protect him. How can this possible be the David and Goliath story? Because of what happens. The mob that wants to kill Tom is described by Scout as, *I looked around the crowd. It was a summer's night, but the men were dressed, most of them, in coveralls and denim shirts buttoned up to the collars. I thought they must be cold-natured, as their sleeves were unrolled and buttoned at the cuffs. Some wore hats pulled firmly down over their ears.*[70] It would be hot and the men are dressed as if they are ready to do some kind of battle. But Scout has a trick up her sleeve. Just as David could not do battle with Goliath on Goliath's terms, Scout takes on the crowd of men ready to kill Tom with simple words of kindness, the opposite of the exchange between David and Goliath. Goliath curses David, *1 Samuel 17:44,45, The Philistine said to David "Come to me, and I will give your flesh to the birds of the air and to the wild animals of the field." But David said to the Philistine, "You come to me with sword and spear and javelin; but I come to you in the name of the Lord of hosts, the God of the armies of Israel, whom you have defied."* Scout is ready to do battle in a similar vein, she compliments Walter Cunningham, *"He's in my grade," I said, " and he does right well. He's a good boy."*[71] In the name of Atticus himself she tackles the mob and continues. *Atticus had said it was the* **polite thing to talk** *to people about what they were interested in, not about what you were interested in. Mr. Cunningham displayed no interest in his son, so I tackled his entailment once more in a last-ditch effort to make him feel at home. "**Entailments are bad**," I was advising him, when I slowly awoke to the fact that I was addressing the entire aggre-gation. The men were all looking at me, some had their mouths half-open. Atticus had stopped poking at Jem: they were standing together beside Dill. Their attention amounted to fascination. Atticus's mouth, even, was half-open, an attitude he had once described as uncouth. Our eyes met and he shut it.*[72] Three little words destroys an entire army of illiterate, hate-filled men bent on murder. I would say that that is a true and believable David and Goliath story, a cartoon of which is in *RJ 25.1 page 17*. Instead of a lynching the gang gets a comeuppance worthy of King David himself. Mr. Cunningham continues, *"Let's clear out," he called. "Let's get going boys."*[73] 1 Samuel 18:50-51, *So David prevailed over the Philistine with a sling and a stone, striking down the Philistine and killing him; there was no sword in David's hand. Then David ran and stood over the Philistine; he grasped his sword, drew it out of its sheath, and killed him; then he cut off his head with it. When the Philistines saw that their champion was dead **they fled.*** Just as Cunningham's mob flees the scene in *TKAM*.

Tom is saved for the moment and our Mr. Underwood is nearby covering the crowd. *Mr. Underwood and a double-barreled shotgun were leaning out of his window above The Maycomb Tribune office.*[74] Underwood sees something pretty good out of his window same as David sees Bathseba in *2 Samuel 11:2&3, It happened, late one afternoon, when David rose from his couch and was walking about on the roof of the king's house, **that he saw from the roof a woman bathing;** the woman was very beautiful. David sent someone to inquire about the woman. It was reported, "This is Bathsheba daughter of Eliam, the wife of Uriah the Hittite."* David has sex with Bathseba and she is soon with his child. David then gets Uriah, Bathseba's husband drunk on wine (this is the reason Underwood has wine at the ready) to try to get him to sleep with his wife Bathseba to hide David's sin of adultery. That did not work out so well for David. Uriah refuses to sleep with his wife as his men in the field have no such comfort. David had Uriah sent to the front of the battle knowing he would be killed. David is guilty of Uriah's death to hide his sin of adultery, matching and mirroring Tom Robinson's death to hide the sin of seduction of a black man in the south by Mayella Ewell.

But Lee is so gifted she can get more than one literary allusion in her writing. And get in a New Testament story as well. Someone else is saved from a self-righteous mob with only a few words and it involves a woman caught in adultery, same as Mayella Ewell. Jesus in *John 8:4-9, they said to him,"Teacher, this woman was caught in the very act of committing adultery. Now in the law of Moses commanded us to stone such a women. Now what do you say?" They said this to test him, so that they might have some charge to bring against him. Jesus bent down and wrote with his finger on the ground. When they kept questioning him, he straightened up and said to them, "Let anyone among you who is without sin be the first to throw a stone at her." And once again he bent down and wrote on the ground. When they heard it, they went away, one by one, beginning with the elders; and Jesus was left alone with the woman standing before him.* David kills Goliath with a single stone and not a single stone is cast against this woman. This pertains to *TKAM* in that the before the kids get to the courthouse they should have been able to see Atticus's sign,

Looking down the hall, we should have seen **Atticus Finch, Attorney at Law** *in the small sober letters agains the light from behind his door.*[75] Since they **do not** see these letters this corresponds to the words that Jesus writes on the ground but are not recorded. The kids cannot read the sign and we cannot know what Jesus writes in the ground. Someone accused of a crime is saved with mere words by Scout and Jesus, both disperse hate-filled crowds bent on murder in the name of righteousness with simple words of kindness, truth and forgiveness.

The story of Joseph in *Genesis* also includes forgiveness for him and his brothers. *TKAM* has a similar story that can be gleaned from Lee's words and directly from the Bible. *Genesis 37:8-9, His brothers said to him, "Are you indeed to reign over us? Are you indeed to have dominion over us?" So they hated him even more because of his dreams and his word. He had another dream, and told it to his brothers saying, "Look, I have had another dream: the sun, the moon, and eleven stars were bowing down to me."* Joseph's brothers later strip him, throw him in a well and then sell him into slavery. Lee's use of this story starts out by stating; *Molasses buckets appeared from nowhere, and the ceiling danced with metallic light.*[76] Very similar to the stars that shine for Joseph. Walter Cunngingham has *no food* for lunch and Scout gets into trouble when she informs the teacher Miss Caroline of this fact. Corresponding to the famine in the land of Canaan that the brothers of Joseph experience. They must travel to Egypt to buy food. Unbeknowst to them their brother Joseph has become second only to Pharaoh in Egypt. Joseph survives an accusation of rape by his master's wife, the opposite of Tom Robinson's plight. Jem invites Walter back to his house for lunch, but not before Scout is punished by Miss Caroline. This is a critical passage, we will see it again at the most perilous of circumstances in *TKAM;* **spitting as a means of sealing oral agreements**. Miss Caroline to Scout, *"You're starting off on the wrong foot in every way, my dear. Hold out your hand." I thought she was going to spit in it, which was the only reason anybody in Maycomb held out his hand; it was a time-honored method of sealing oral contracts. Wondering what bargain we had made, I turned to the class for an answer, but the class looked back at me in puzzlement.[77]* Scout later beats up Walter Cunningham and rubs his face in the dirt for getting her off on the wrong foot. This corresponds to the brothers throwing Joseph into a well.

But at lunch with the Finches, Walter and Atticus talk like grown men, Jem and Scout are amazed, just as the brothers are amazed when they are seated in birth order before they know that their brother Joseph is indeed lord over them. *Genesis 43:33, When they were seated before him, the firstborn according to his birthright and the youngest according to his youth, the men looked at one another in* **amazement**. Walter piles on the food just as Benjamin is given fives time the amount of food on his plate, *Genesis 43:34. Portions were taken to them from Joseph's table, but Benjamin's portion was* *five times as much as any of theirs.* Back to *TKAM, While Walter piled food on his plate, he and Atticus talked together like two men, to the wonderment of Jem and me. Atticus was expounding upon farm problems when Walter interrupted to ask if there was any molasses in the house. Atticus summoned Calpurnia, who returned bearing the syrup pitcher. She stood waiting for Walter to help himself. Walter poured syrup on his vegetables and meat with a generous hand. He would probably have poured it into his milk had I not asked what the sam hill he was doing. The silver saucer clattered when he replaced the pitcher, and he quickly put his hands in his lap. Then he ducked his head.*[78] It is not the syrup but the ***silver saucer*** that is the hero in this scene. Drowning his food with the syrup and clattering the silver saucer represents something he should not do, or "returning evil for good", why else hang your head in shame? *Genesis 44:1-5, Then he (Joseph) commanded the steward of his house, "Fill the men's sack with food, as much as they can carry, and put each man's money in the top of his sack. Put my cup, the silver cup, in the top of the sack of the youngest, with his money for the grain." And he did as Joseph told him. As soon as the morning was light, the men were sent away with their donkeys. When they had gone only a short distance from the city, Joseph said to his steward, "Go follow after the men and when you overtake them, say to them, '**Why have you returned evil for good? Why have you stolen my silver cup?** Is it not from this that my lord drinks? Does he not indeed use it for divination? You have done wrong in doing this.'"* Scout is relegated to the kitchen to finish eating mirroring the brothers as they take their food back to Canaan. Scout gets admonished by Calpurnia for the way Scout treats company and later tells Scout to *"Hush your fussin" she (Calpurnia)said.*[79] Just so as the brothers are leaving Egypt Joseph gets in the exact same dressing-down, *Genesis 45:24, Then he sent his brothers on their way, and as they were leaving he said to them, "Do not quarrel along the way."*

If we are exposing characters to their Biblical counterparts, here is another one that may otherwise slip through the cracks. Harper Lee has X Billups declaring verbally his name, *X,* in court. No one believes him so, finally X must write it down and hold it up to declare it to the world. How else to proclaim His Name? So too Jesus states in John 17:26, *"And I declare to them your name, and will declare it, that the love with which You loved Me may be in them, and I in them."* The triumphant Jesus has to enter Jerusalem on Palm Sunday before any trial can begin, right? So how to do it in *TKAM?* He must enter on a donkey so X Billups is on a mule the off-spring of a donkey and a horse. Now, *X* in Greek is the letter *chi,* this being the first letter of Christ in Greek. Harper Lee was a Chi Omega at Alabama. The first letter of his second name starts with B. The **second** letter of Christ in Greek is *P, rho,* and by simply dropping the lower part of the B you get a P. The combination of the two letters X, and P is the symbol for Christ. Though she could have someone named X Phillips or such, P is not the second letter of our alphabet and it is not secretive and devilishly clever enough for Lee. The **triumphant** Christ is only seen one time on Palm Sunday; our *TKAM* counterpart Mr. X Billups is never heard from again in *TKAM*. But a Mr. X can be found in a *Rammer Jammer 25.5 page 10.*

To continue with Mr. Dill Harris, he gets some special treatment from a character that I need to reintroduce; Dolphus Raymond, who in the Biblical *TKAM* is John the Baptist. Why is Dolphus Raymond John the Baptist? First is his name; Dolphus, no one else has that name. And John is named John even though no one else in his family has that name. *Luke 1:59-63, On the eighth day they came to circumcise the child, and they were going to name him Zechariah after his father. But his mother said, "No; he is to be called John." They said to her, "None of your relatives has this name." He asked for a writing tablet and wrote, "His name is John." And all of them were amazed.* But it gets even better with the meaning of Dolphus. It is short for Adolphus, which means *noble wolf.* And we all know wolves cry out in the wilderness. What does John the Baptist call himself? *John 1:22-23, Then they said to him, "Who are you? Let us have an answer for those who sent us. What do you say about yourself?" He said, "I am the voice of one crying out in the wilderness, 'Make straight the way of the Lord'"* as the prophet Isaiah said.

Dolphus Raymond is not trash as Dill notes and Jem declares, *"He's not, he owns all one side of the riverbank down there, and he's from a real old family."*[80] In *Matthew 3:9*, John is associated with the oldest of Hebrew families, "*And do not think to say to yourselves, 'We have Abraham as our father.' For I say to you that God is able to raise up children to Abraham from these stones.*" We all know John baptizes Jesus in the river Jordan, *Matthew 3:13.* One more definition and maybe the gentle reader can catch my drift. Dolphus Raymond is thought to be caught in the throes of the whisky hell he drinks when he comes into town. Whisky came to us from the Old Irish/Scottish Gaelic as *water of life.* Recall that only Dill drinks from the bottle and we have only one baptism for the forgiveness of sins. He lives with a black woman and wears the only English riding boots in Maycomb County. Scout likes his smell. "*You mean all you drink in that is Coca-Cola? Just plain Coca-Cola?" Yes ma'am," Mr. Raymond nodded. I liked his smell: it was of leather, horses, cottonseed. He wore the only English riding boots I had ever seen.*[81] This is significant. John the Baptist is known to eat wild honey and wear leather. *Matthew 3:4, Now John wore clothing of camel's hair with a leather belt around his waist, and his food was locusts and wild honey.* I think it is fair to say that a black girlfriend in 1935 Alabama would be considered a "**wild honey**" and clothing of camel hair is the opposite of English riding boots just as Nelle is the opposite of Ellen.

Dolphus Raymond continues to relate to the children, when Scout asks, "*Why do you do like you do?*"

"*Wh-oh yes, you mean why do I pretend? Well, it's very simple.*" he said. "*Some folks don't -like the way I live. Now I* could say the hell with 'em, I don't care if they don't like it. I do say I don't care if they don't like it, right enough-but I don't say the hell with 'em see?"

Dill and I said, "No sir."

"I try to give 'em a reason, you see. It helps folks if they can latch onto a reason. When I come to town, which is seldom, if I weave a little and drink out of this sack, folks can say Dolphus Raymond's in the clutches of whisky-that's why he won't change his ways. He can't help himself, that's why he lives the way he does."

"That ain't honest, Mr. Raymond, making yourself out **badder** than you are already--"

"It ain't honest but it's mighty helpful to folks. Secretly, Miss Finch, I'm not much of a drinker, but you see they could never, never understand that I live like I do because that's the way I want to live."

I had a feeling that I shouldn't be here listening to this sinful man who had mixed children and didn't care who knew it, but he was fascinating. I had never encountered a being who deliberately perpetrated a fraud against himself. But why had he entrusted us with his deepest secret? I asked him why.

"Because you're children and you can understand it," **he said, "and because I heard that one-"**

He jerked his head at Dill: "Things haven't caught up with that one's instinct yet. Let him get a little older and he won't get sick and **cry**.

"Cry about what, Mr. Raymond?" Dill's maleness was beginning to assert itself.

"*Cry about the simple hell people give other people--without even thinking. Cry about the hell white people give colored folks, without even stopping to think that they're people too.*"[82]

The Bible is quite evident in *TKAM*, Lee to me seems inspired by this passage in *Luke* chapter 7. Corresponding to *Proverbs 7* that is a mirror of the *TKAM* story.

*Luke 7:31-35, "To what then will I compare the people of this generation and what are they like? They are like children sitting in the marketplace and calling to one another, 'We played the flute for you, and you did not dance; we **wailed** and **you did not weep**.' For John the Baptist has come eating no bread and drinking **no wine**, and you say, '**He has a demon**'; the Son of Man has come eating and drinking, and you say, 'Look, a glutton and a drunkard, a friend of tax collectors and sinners!' Nevertheless, **wisdom is vindicated by all her children.**"*

I think that these stories connect and intertwine to bolster my theory that Lee is rewriting the Bible and that the Pageant in *TKAM* is the Passion of the Christ. And that several things indicate this, the lack of any crosses in Calpurnia's church or the happy cemetery, the fact that Atticus calls the year 1935 **a year of grace**, and **not** *year of our Lord*, and that an educated person does not know why Jew's are persecuted, indicating to me that the only reason for this is that the Passion and Crucifixion of Christ has yet to happen in *To Kill a Mockingbird*. And that Scout in the ham outfit will represent Him on the Cross. With Jem as he is rendered unconscious is the entombed Christ and Boo Radley is the Risen Christ.

CHAPTER 6

The only reason Lee is able to write *Go Set a Watchman* then *To Kill a Mockingbird* is that she is loaned money on Christmas day of 1956. The Browns are her good friends do this as they have faith in her and want her to succeed. She is loaned enough money for one year off by the Browns the exact amount is not known. However much it is it does the job and we have enjoyed her work ever since. But again, more is there than meets the eye. Christmas was a special time of the year for the *Rammer Jammer* staff. But of course, little was off limits and Santa Claus and other Christmas showcases were made fun of. In the *Rammer Jammer* Christmas issues there are parodies of *Twas the Night Before Christmas* and Lee herself wrote a spoof of the *Yes, Virginia, There is a Santa Claus* letter from the *New York Sun* of September 21, 1897, by Virginia O'Hanlon. I think I have established that there are connections to be made within *TKAM* and Lee hides things well within the words themselves as she incorporates *Proverbs 25.2* throughout the book. She wants to put some reference to Christmas but hide it in the words, phrases and numbers themselves. She has the time, money and genius to do this and get away with it. There is simply another story within a story going on in *TKAM*. I found no satire of the song *The Twelve Days of Christmas* in any *Rammer Jammer* and I have looked at every one. Therefore, I will make a fearless attempt to demonstrate that that minx surreptitiously wrote words that are the rough counterpart, sometimes very rough, to *The Twelve Days of Christmas*. And she does it in both *To Kill a Mockingbird* and *Go Set a Watchman*. This will be presented backwards just like her name is backward of Ellen, starting with *Twelve Drummers Drumming* in chapter four. The same chapter that introduces us to *Proverbs 25.2*, the kids playing rather than listening to *One Man's Family, Chapter XXV, Book II*. The kids are doing something different with the show that most would not do, just as Lee is playing a cat and mouse game with her words. Lee will end with a *Partridge in a Pear Tree* in chapter twelve corresponding to Christmas in the twelfth month.

One day we were so busily playing Chapter XXV, Book II of One Man's Family, we did not see Atticus standing on the sidewalk looking at us, slapping a rolled magazine against his knee. The sun said **twelve** *noon.*

"What are you playing?" he asked.

"Nothing," said Jem.

Jem's evasion told me our game was a **secret, so I kept quiet**.

"What are you doing with those scissors, then? Why are you tearing up that newspaper? If it's today's I'll tan you."[83]

And just as Scout says she will keep quiet about it; I think that this is Lee talking to herself through Scout to keep silent about this internal secret and risky game she is playing. As an unknown writer producing her first book this may have been no big deal if it had middling success which she probably thought it would. She may have even thought that once out of print she could divulge this secret and spur more sales. But for a Pulitzer Prize winning book it is something completely different to reveal that the words representing this song are within *TKAM*. Had it come out she may have been embarrassed about this being within award-winning *TKAM*. This discreetness accompanies her *Proverb 25.2* theme. Too much is on the line to reveal a parody or spoof is within the extraordinary words of *TKAM*. Readers would simply want to know what else is within and boy is there a mountain of secrets to reveal as I am attempting to do now. Not the least of which is that I believe that *rolled* should be read as *Roll Tide* the University of Alabama cheer that brings on hives to Notre Dame Fans. And the *magazine* could be read as the *Rammer Jammer* magazine and *slapping* means *drumming*. *RJ 16.1, page 20* notes that skins which are of course *tanned* are drums, i.e. **Twelve Drummers Drumming**. Lee writes *twelve noon* instead of just noon to imply, in my opinion, that there are two things going on here.

Towards the end of *TKAM* Scout notes that they will have to learn algebra. As I pursue the secrets within, this is a clue to the inner workings of the secrets within *TKAM*.

Math must be used in order to reveal some mysteries. If, in Chapter Five you add up, 5 o'clock bath, 2nd Battle of the Marne, 3-inch-high nut grass and 1 exception, you get the **eleven** for *11 Pipers Piping* with Miss Maudie. *Miss Maudie hated her house: time spent indoors was time wasted. She was a widow, a chameleon lady who worked in her flower beds in an old straw hat and men's coveralls, but after her **five** o'clock bath she would appear on the porch and reign over the street in magisterial beauty. She loved everything that grew in God's earth, even the weeds. With **one** exception. If she found a blade of nut grass in her yard it was like the **Second** Battle of the Marne: she would swoop down upon it with **a tin tub** and subject it to blasts from beneath with a **poisonous substance** she said would be so powerful it'd kill us all if we didn't stand far away. "Why can't you just pull it up?" I asked after witnessing a prolonged campaign against a blade not **three** inches high.*[84] The sound *of 11 Pipers Piping* would be excruciatingly loud, almost a *poisonous substance*, and *tin tub will roughly represent pipes*

Thankfully, the easiest one is next for both *GSAW* and *TKAM*. In *GSAW* Chapter Five, **Ten Lords a Leaping**, has the lord of the underworld doing the honors. *Hell was and would always be as far as she was concerned, a lake of fire exactly the size of Maycomb, Alabama, surrounded be a brick wall two hundred feet high. Sinners were **pitchforked over this wall by Satan,** and they simmered throughout eternity in a sort of broth of liquid sulfur.*[85] The numbers on this page can add up to ten but she puts in more than needed as her smokescreen.

In *TKAM; Dill and Jem emerged from a brief huddle: "If you stay you've got to do what we tell you," Dill warned. "We-ll," I said, "who's so **high and mighty** all of a sudden?" "If you don't say you'll do what we tell you, we ain't gonna tell you anything," Dill continued. "You act like **you grew ten** inches in the night! All right what is it?"*[86] **Ten Lords-A-Leaping** that's what. *Lords* are *high and mighty* and growing suddenly **ten** inches is close to *leaping.* Neither Scout nor Nelle tell anything about her secret. I unfortunately cannot say the same.

But I can say that I like **Nine Ladies Dancing** the best. Chapter 6 has a quite the display by Mr. Avery. *There was a **lady** in the moon in Maycomb. She sat at a dresser combing her hair. "We're gonna miss you, boy," I said. "Reckon we better watch for Mr. Avery?" Mr. Avery boarded across the street from Mrs. Henry Lafayette Dubose's house. Besides making change in the collection plate every Sunday, Mr. Avery sat on the porch every night until **nine** o'clock and sneezed. One evening we were privileged to **witness a performance** (read dancing) by him which seemed to have been his positively last, for he never did it again so long as we watched. … a closer inspection revealed an arc of water descending from the leaves and splashing in a yellow circle of the street light, some ten feet from source to earth, it seemed to us. Dill said he must drink a gallon a day, and the ensuing contest to determine relative distance and respective prowess only made me feel left out again, as I was untalented in this area.*[87]

Lee's paean to ***Nine Ladies Dancing***. With a feat that would make any man bust his buttons. And a perfect example of Lee's artistry with words. If your analysis is correct, Avery is passing water, but this is only alluded to, never named. Where else to find a lady in the moon but at *MOONWINX Sandwich Shoppe* in *Rammer Jammer Volume 14 Number 1*.[88]

I will avoid noting the **nine** with the arrow pointing right at it as that might be considered a bit redundant.

Besides, *RJ Volume 4 Number 1* also has a lady at her dresser in the appropriately named *Hay Fever* issue; "**Not to be sneezed at**"[89], not even by Mr. Avery at nine.

Our very first *Rammer Jammer Volume 1 Number 1, page 29* has drinking involved and a *Lady Moon* passing all of us. But not passing in the manner Avery is passing, I think.

Ok, this one may be on the rough side. ***8 Maids-a-Milking***. A bit of a stretch but here goes. "*...now in 1864, when Stonewall Jackson came around by---I beg your pardon, young folks. Ol' Blue Light was in heaven then, God rest his saintly brow...*"[90] The **8** in 1864 counts for our number.

With this in mind, I faced Cecil Jacobs, in the school-yard next day: "*You gonna take that back boy?*" "*You gotta make me first!*" *he yelled.* "*My folks said your daddy was a disgrace an' that n---- oughta hang from the* **water-tank**!"[91] The *water* in water-tank refers to a drink, so it counts for *milking*. But to those into my way of thinking about *TKAM* the *cow* in cow-ard gives it all away. *I drew a bead on him, remembered what Atticus had said, then* ***dropped my fists*** *and walked away,*

"Scout's a **cow--ward!**" *ringing in my ears. It was the first time I ever walked away from a fight.*[92] Scout drops her fists and walks away first time from a fight thus our **maid;** Atticus *made* her stop her fighting ways. How else to milk a cow but with teats in *fists and dropping* same. I would not know from personal experience. A water tower is depicted in *RJ 1.3, page 8* in an appropriately named *"Women's Issue"*.

Lee even recycles Virginia O'Hanlon's name in *Go Set a Watchman*; *"Gentlemen, our speaker for today is Mr. Grady O'Hanlon. He needs no introduction. Mr. O'Hanlon rose and said, "As the cow said to the milkman on a cold morning, 'Thank you for the warm hand.'"*[93] If you count the nearby numbers, they equal **8**, for ***Eight Maids a Milking***, and it is in chapter eight of *GSAW*. This adds weight to the argument that the chapter numbers are noteworthy, as the snow in *TKAM* falls in chapter eight and eight inches of snow is recorded falling in *RJ 23.4*. The fact that numbers in and of themselves are significant is epitomized by the preceding passage in *GSAW*. *The courthouse clock creaked, strained, said, "Phlugh!" and struck the hour. Two. When the sound shivered away she saw her father rise and address the assembly in his dry courtroom voice:*[94] The *"Two"* is masquerading as a sentence all by itself, in fact without any *verb* **it is not** a sentence. It means to me that the *numbers* are a feature by themselves with their own set of secret rules and regulations, that will flow seamlessly into *TKAM* and help cement my theory that Lee is writing far more than what we read and that *Proverbs 25.2* is almost constantly in the back of her head.

Seven Swans-a-Swimming is probably the roughest. Scout gets into a fight, as she cannot keep from fighting forever. The *seven* red marks is our number and eight is camouflage. Lee is, of course, well aware of what she is doing and needs to conceal her intentions. *When I surveyed the damage there were only **seven** or eight red marks.*[95] She *sails* into said fight and gets arms pinned, just as a swan has its wings on its sides and *sailed in* stands in for **swimming**. *This time, I split my knuckle to the bone on his front teeth. My left impaired, I **sailed in** with my right, but not for long. Uncle Jack **pinned my arms to my sides** and said, "Stand still!"*[96] But the piece of resistance is Scout looking at a tiny ant "struggling" with a bread crumb in the grass. *I found myself suddenly looking at a **tiny ant** struggling with a bread crumb in the grass.*[97] Small could be substituted for tiny; add one of Lee's ubiquitous hyphens, lose some letters and you have **sm-an**. Oh, turn the *m* upside down and you have instant **Swan**. Lee uses *struggling*, I think, to show just how difficult these allusions and metaphors are for her. I wonder if it is at this point, she throws it all out the window as it is such a strain. Even Victor Hugo says something similar in *Les Misérables. One day he actually twisted an ankle trying to avoid treading on an ant.*[98]

RJ Volume 29 Number 7, page 12 evinces writing upside down is not only possible but preferable.

Six Geese-a-Laying is laid out in Chapter Eleven. *It was only* **three forty-five** *(5+4-3= 6)* *when we got home, so Jem and I drop-kicked in the back yard until it was time to meet Atticus. Atticus had two* **yellow** *pencils for me and a* **football** *magazine for Jem, which I suppose was a* **silent reward** *for our first day's session with Mrs. Dubose.*[99] Failure to score in football can be called getting *a goose egg* instead of a zero. Since they have no goal posts there would be no scoring. So, footballs are eggs, and *silent reward* is laying of footballs. There is an article from *RJ Volume 22 Number 3, page 27* that associates football with geese eggs, and we all know how much laying down a touchdown is worth (6). Scout and Jem drop-kick in *TKAM* you can bet that it is mentioned in *Rammer Jammer 5.2 page 15 and in RJ 8.2 on page 22.*

Chapter 11**,** **Five Golden Rings***,* is worse than rough. To hide *golden,* she uses *rose,* it is the only color mentioned, *Jem* **rose.** *"But--"*[100] Additionally, there is such a thing as **rose gold***,* I found it on the internet, so it has to be true. *"Do you know what time it is, Atticus?" she said. "Exactly fourteen minutes past* **five***. The alarm clock's set for five-thirty. I want you to know that."*[101] And here is why; *The alarm clock was the signal for our release; if one day it did not* **ring***, what would we do?*[102] Keep singing Scout, keep singing, only four more verses to go. To **not ring** is the opposite of *ring,* so it counts for my wicked way of thinking.

Chapter 12, more algebra for our **Four-Calling-Birds***.* And almost as easy to understand as *Ten Lords a-Leaping.*

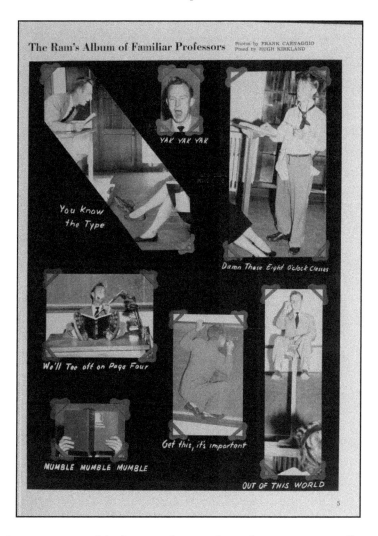

Scout is miserable for *two* days without her permanent fiancé, Dill. Plus, Atticus is in emergency session of the state legislature for *two* weeks. And the kids are just as surprised as Lee is by the way she manipulates her way into this one. *We were surprised one morning to see a cartoon in The Montgomery Advertiser above the caption, "Maycomb's Finch." It showed*

Atticus barefooted and in short pants, chained to a desk: he was diligently writing on a slate while some frivolous-looking girls yelled, "Yoo-hoo!" at him.[103] Our Professor in *RJ 25.2* [104]thinks this is so important, he too is writing it on a **slate**.

A trifle sexist but girls are also called *birds*. See picture below from *Rammer Jammer Volume 22-Number 4.*[105]

RJ Volume 16 number 6 has a *four calling birds*, frivolous or not, yelling *You Hoo, Willie!*[106] If you think Lee uses the word *frivolous* randomly you will have to think again. In Henry James's, *The Portrait of a Lady*, the word has a bond with birds; "**Frivolous rebukes**" is an expression used to criticize someone. The statement means, according to the situation, that "*the author's grandmother criticized or checked on the **sparrows**, in vain.*" *Looking* and *checked on* are certainly remarkably similar. And our girls in *TKAM* (*4 calling birds*) seem to be criticizing Atticus at least a little. So, birds and frivolous go together like words of a feather, supporting my thesis and keeping Nelle Harper Lee in the Researchers Hall of Fame. There is not one, but I would nominate Lee to be first award winner.

Three French Hens is in the same chapter twelve that records both *Mardi Gras*, French for Fat Tuesday, the day before Ash Wednesday the start of Lent to prepare for Easter and the Passion of Christ. the *Quarter (French)* that blacks live in and Tom Robinson's wife Helen's (***Hens***) ***three*** *lit-tle'uns*. *"It's like we were going to **Mardi Gras**," said Jem. "What's all this for, Cal?"* Scout: *My curiosity burst: "Why were*

*you takin' up col-lection for Tom Robinson's wife?" "Didn't you hear why?" asked Reverend Sykes. "**Hel-en's got three little'uns** and she can't go to work-"[107]* I think that the hyphens equal more hidden messages, as Helen enigmatically has *3 little'uns,* rather than children. French hens typically do not have children. Taking out the *e* and the *l* from *Helen's* and it **becomes** *Hens.* Restructuring words in this manner would be a prize winner in a word contest from *RJ 25.2, page 20.* During the attack after the pageant, when the kids think that it is Cecil Jacobs after them, the word *hen* is used **three times.** Any insult word could have been used any number of times, but Lee purposefully uses **hen three** times building my argument for me.

She gets in the ***Two Turtle Doves*** in two different places. Forget not that ***One-Shot Finch*** leaves ***one* dove** alive in chapter ten, shooting fourteen out of fifteen. *Doves* used here instead of ducks, quail or pigeons helps prove my premise. Chapter one has turtle talk, and an admonition to think a little. *"Dill you have to think about these things," Jem said. "Lemme think a minute ... it's sort of like making a **turtle** come*

DEDDY! WHERE HEV YOU BIN OL DEAS YEARS?

out…"[108] Jem, Dill and Harper Lee succeeded in getting me to think.

Calpurnia celebrates her birthday on Christmas, and we conclude our *Twelve Days of Christmas.* It is no coincidence that it ends in the *twelfth* chapter of *TKAM.* First recall that Link Deas (give me a break; read *Link These* as did our cartoonist from *RJ 28.3[109]*; **Deas** in place of *these*) has pecan *trees.* Helen will work picking them. *Reverend Sykes hesitated. "To tell the truth, Miss Jean Louise, Helen's finding it hard to get work these days … when it's picking time, I think Mr.* **Link Deas***'ll take her."[110]* Pecan trees are not nut trees, but a type of *fruit* called a drupe, just as a *pear* tree is fruit tree. All the more reason Link Deas does not have apple, peach or pear trees; just using the name *Link Deas* counts for our *tree* and more *Proverbs 25.2* camouflage. *Jem said it looked like they could save the collection money for a year* (twelve months*) and get some hymn-books.[111]* They go to *First Purchase* [112] as in purchasing gifts. Cal is older than Mr. Finch; *Finch* standing in for *partridge* as Lee could just as easily written Atticus, but that would not have fulfilled her purpose of getting in a substitute for *partridge.* She expounds on the lesser qualities' men have over women, *"I'm older than Mr.* **Finch,** *even."* Calpurnia grinned. *"Not sure how much, though. We started rememberin' one time, trying to figure out how old I was - I can remember back just a few years more'n he can, so I'm not much older, when you take off the fact that* **men** *can't remember as well as* **women.***"[113]* Cal grins as she knows the scoop, secret message and all. *Men* and *women* count for our **pair for Partridge in a Pear Tree.** In sum, *Finch* equals **Partridge**, men and women are the pair/**Pear** and Link Deas's fruit **Trees** (pecans prominent in *RJ 22.5 page 12*)links these all up in a nice package ready to be opened about sixty years or so after they are written.

*"I just have it on **Christmas**, it's easier to remember that way-I don't have a real birthday."*[114] Cal states.

Neither do we know the real birthday of the Christ; we just celebrate by giving gifts; with Santa Claus doing the honors. And Nelle Harper Lee concealing the best gift giving song within *TKAM*.

Because there is one clue to the *Twelve Days of Christmas* that almost escaped me. It is so subtle and silent that it could be compared to a single flap of a butterfly's wing. And again, it is the opposite or reverse of the joy and peace that Christmas brings. War. Bob Ewell is a veteran of an "***obscure war***".[115] There is only one candidate for this and that is the Negro Rebellion in Cuba in the year 1912. The indication or clue is that this war is also nicknamed simply ***The Twelve***. Harper Lee can insert her hints in vastly differing and imaginative ways, and I think this one leads us to the fact that she did insert a parody of ***The Twelve*** *Days of Christmas* into *TKAM*. It follows her modus operandi of reversing the metaphors and it is so well hidden it complements her *Proverbs 25.2* theme, *It is the glory of God to conceal things; but the glory of kings is to search things out.* I hope that this can be believed.

But if it is thought otherwise and that this is cobbled together with duck-tape and bubblegum out of whole cloth, I think that is the exact point. Only by doing said cobbling, bubble-gumming, duck taping and cage-rattling thinking like Jem tells us to could anyone come up with this little theory.

CHAPTER 7

Every artist needs some inspiration, model, or references to pull from. Lee seems to be drawing hers from primarily the *Rammer Jammer* at the University of Alabama, the *Bible* and *Les Misérables.* Due to the amount of stimulus she receives one can conjecture that the only true way for her to hide it is to never talk about it, lest her secrets are revealed and her status and esteem in certain small minded circles might suffer. Maybe even sales drop off as readers dig into her source material rather than the story itself. She obviously cares nothing for celebrity unlike her friend Truman Capote. In fact, she seems to loath it. But her creative genius is far more than the inspiration she receives even if there are parallels, connections, and links to be made, she is personally, almost existentially connected to her sources of inspiration, such as our Bishop Bienvenu the Catholic priest that saves Jean Valjean in *Les Misérables,* as well as Cosette and Jean Valjean himself. Jean Valjean is, of course, noted in *RJ 16.3 page 18.*

Bienvenu means *welcome* in French. *Les Misérables, Part One, Book One, Chapter Two, ...among all the bishop's various names that made the most sense to them, and so they called him Monseigneur Bienvenu – Welcome. Besides the nickname tickled him.*[116] In *Part One, Book One, Chapter Six*, Bishop Welcome states, *"The finest alter is the* **soul** *of some poor wretch who finds comfort and gives thanks to God."*[117] Chapter nine of *TKAM*, Welcome Finch, the **sole** son is introduced. *There were six bedrooms upstairs, four for the eight female children, one for Welcome Finch, the* **sole** *son, and one for visiting relatives. Simple enough; but the daughters' room could be reached only by one staircase, Welcome's room and the guestroom only by another. The Daughters' Staircase was in the ground-floor bedroom of their parents, so Simon knew the hours of his daughters' nocturnal comings and goings.*[118] Welcome Finch is never mentioned again. He could have been called the only or lone or even the one, but Lee deliberately uses a word that sounds like **soul**. I doubt if even the Library of Congress has any other books with **Welcome** as a character name, with significance for the **soul/sole**. And they both probably wore shoes so we can include shoe soles.

The connections are far more personal to Harper Lee than just names and homonyms. Lee's gift on Christmas gives her a new beginning; same with Cosette in *Les Misérables*. She is bought from the Thénardiers by Jean Valjean on Christmas day. Too evil for even Dickens this repugnant, squalid couple show up here. The price is fifteen hundred francs, which may roughly be equivalent to the sum Lee received on Christmas day that gave her a new start and hope for a much better day with more sunshine, great writing and good times. Christmas is essential to Jean Valjean, Cosette and Nelle Harper Lee in such a way that means new life itself. Both Cosette and Scout receive dolls from their benefactor and savior. Cosette's doll lives in *Part Two, Book Three, Chapter Four* of *Les Misérables*; Hugo mentions that Cosette takes a *furtive* look at the doll's beautiful silky hair, just like Lee notes that Scout's doll that Boo Radley gives her has bangs just like her.

Atticus is the best shot but we have someone else that can shoot pretty well; Jean Valjean, in *Les Misérables, Part One, Book Five, Chapter Three; He liked to carry a gun on his walks but he rarely used it. When he did so, **his aim** was **infallible** and it frightened people. He never killed an animal that wasn't dangerous. **He never fired at any small bird**.*[119] Chapter ten of *TKAM* has the seminal statement not to shoot mockingbirds, *Atticus said to Jem one day, "I'd rather you shot at tin cans in the back yard, but I know you'll go after birds. Shoot all the bluejays you want, if you can hit 'em, but remember it's a sin to kill a mockingbird.*[120] *Les Misérables* in *Part One, Book Two, Chapter Six; He had a gun, which he could use **better than any marksman in the world**.*[121] With Lee's prodigious ability to do research, coincidences can, for all practical purposes, be rule out. Because there are more connections to *Les Misérables*. In *TKAM*, Sir Walter Scott is transformed into *Sir Walter Scout*[122]; Lord Byron gets the same treatment in *Part*

One, Book Three, Chapter One, Lord Byron was beginning to shine; a note in a poem of Millevoye's introduced him to France as "a certain Lord Baron."[123] And if Lee can say it with flowers so can Hugo. At the end of *Les Misérables, Part Five, Book Nine, Chapter Five*, Jean Valjean states, *"I'm going to die in a little while."[124]* A handful of paragraphs prior, Cosette states, *"…The azaleas are coming along nicely."[125]* And we all know Miss Maudie loves her azaleas; however, they are so toxic that getting a bouquet of them was a sleep with the fishes' threat. *Wikipedia: Azaleas and rhododendrons were once so infamous for their toxicity that to receive a bouquet of their flowers in a black vase was a well-known death threat.*

By some magic of mathematical and literary license, algebra is mentioned in both books. I am sure finding such a word in many other books is common, but I doubt that they have this kind of depth and connectivity. *Part Four, Book Three, Chapter Three* of *Les Misérables,* **Algebra** *applies to the clouds; the radiance of the star benefits the rose. …Light does not carry off earthly perfumes into the blue without knowing what it does with them; night distributes stellar essence to the sleeping flowers. All the* **birds** *that fly hold the thread of infinity in their claws.[126]* Chapter 31 of *TKAM*, after the attack and Jem is alive and Ewell is dead, Scout states, *The street lights were fuzzy from the fine rain that was falling. As I made my way home, I felt very old … As I made my way home, I thought Jem and I would get grown but there wasn't much else left for us to learn, except possibly* **algebra.**[127]

Like numbers themselves, connections will not stop, Lee's first attempt is found and published as *Go Set a **Watchman*** from *Isaiah 21:6.* In *Les Misérables, Part One, Book One, Chapter Six, The bishop put his hand on the man's shoulder with a gentle gravity and said to him from the Psalms (127:1): Except the Lord keep the house the **watchman** waketh but in vain.*[128] As previously stated, families in Maycomb County are judged by their bonds back to the Battle of Hasting in 1066; the Norman invasion of England. Chapter one of *TKAM; Being Southerners, it was a source of shame to some members of the family that we had no recorded ancestors on either side of the Battle of Hastings.*[129] *RJ 25.2, page 5* also has a reference to that battle; William the Conqueror was also called the Bastard King of England. Similarly, *Part One, Book One, Chapter Nine* of *Les Misérables, They are really and truly **a very old Norman family** from the Caen region. They go back five hundred years to a Raoul de Faux, a **Jean** de Faux, and a Thomas de Faux, who were all noblemen, one of them being a seigneur de Rochefort. His **daughter**, Marie-**Louise**, married Adrien-Charles de Gramont…*[130] Lee may have even generated Scout's first name from this passage as both *Jean* and *Louise* are evinced.

Atticus in chapter eight saves something very valuable from the fire at Miss Maudie's house. *I saw Atticus carrying Miss Maudie's heavy oak rocking chair, and thought it sensible of him to save what she valued most.*[131] It is about as shocking as a stripper at a bachelor party to know that Jean Valjean does something similar in *Part One, Book Five, Chapter One* of *Les Misérables, ... as night was closing in on a cold December day, with a knapsack on his back and a thorn stuck in his hand, a great fire had just broken out in the community hall. The man had thrown himself into the blaze and, at the risk of his own life, had saved two children who turned out to belong to the captain of the gendarmerie-which meant that no one thought to ask him for his passport.*[132] As a convict, to Jean Valjean, anonymity is more valuable than gold or Miss Maudie's old oak chair.

Where she gets the idea to use numbers to foreshadow and develop the characters is beyond compare: Victor Hugo's, *Les Misérables Part One, Book Two, Chapter Three,* Jean Valjean states to the bishop that takes him in when he cannot rent a room for the night that it took 19 years to gain 109 francs and 15 sous. The Bishop repeats, *19 years!* So, using my Biblical decoder ring I find *Proverbs 19:19, A man of great wrath shall suffer punishment: for if you deliver him, yet thou must do it again.* Which is exactly what transpired as the Bishop gives Jean Valjean the two silver candlesticks instead of a telling the gendarmes about the theft of the silverware. *Psalms 109* has *31 verses* and is *Les Misérables* in short. Just like *Proverbs 7* is *TKAM* in microcosm.

More gifts parallel more connections between *TKAM* and *Les Misérables*. In chapter four, here is how Jem discovers the coins from Boo, *"Indian-heads." He said. "Nineteen-six and Scout, one of 'em's from nineteen-hundred. These are real old." "Nineteen-hundred," I echoed. "Say-".*[133] Lee repeats nineteen-hundred in the same fashion as Hugo repeats nineteen; Bishop Bienvenu, *"A hundred and nine franc fifteen sous. And how long did it take you to earn that?"* Jean Valjean, *"Nineteen years" "Nineteen years!" the bishop let out a deep sigh.*[134] Note that Jem says nineteen-six, not nineteen-hundred and six. Recall that Atticus states that they are indeed poor. Reading *Proverbs 19:1&5-6, Better the poor walking in integrity than one perverse of speech who is a fool. A false witness shall not be unpunished, and he that speaketh lies shall not escape. **19:6. Many will intreat the favour of the prince, and everyman is a friend to him that giveth gifts.*** She cannot use nineteen alone as the clue would be much too obvious; almost palpable. Money, years, the number nineteen, *Proverbs*, even the reiterative effect all used in the same context in both books in almost the identical articulation; unquestionably cannot be happenstance or unintentional coincidence. This encourages the existential connection to *Les Misérables*; both have 19 at prominent and important points that lead to the *Old Testament book of Proverbs*. The ability to foreshadow without writing a single word is artistry beyond compare. Nelle Harper Lee's originality with words includes gymnastics with words that is louder than her silence. I hope the reader can hear it like I do. The ability to predict and presage without using words is more amazing every time it appears. But you have to follow the money and make the connection to the real direction the dates or numbers take you.

CHAPTER 8

There is one connection to *Les Misérables* that deserves special attention. Not as the parallel is easy to comprehend, but because it is difficult. Several things have to be drawn together to make this relationship understandable. But it does start with Fantine in *Les Misérables*. She is on her deathbed and shakes uncontrollably right before she dies in *Part 1, Book 8 Chapter 4*. In fact, several of the principle characters in *Les Misérables* shake right before they pass away. Javert's death is foreshadowed by the fact that he shakes right after Fantine's death. Recall for now that Dill predicts that Scout will die in chapter 4 of *TKAM*. He states that she will die in three days the exact opposite of Jesus rising in three days in the Gospels. So why should Jean Louise Finch shake in Chapter 24 of *TKAM?* Let's just say it is the climax of the whole thing. *Had I been attentive, I would have had another scrap to add to Jem's definition of background, but I found myself **shaking** and couldn't stop. I had seen Enfield Prison Farm, and Atticus had pointed out the exercise yard to me. It was the size of a football field. "Stop that shaking," commanded*

Miss Maudie, and I stopped. "Get up, Alexandra, we've left 'em long enough."[135] Simply put, it is her time in the Garden of Gethsemane, that is why Lee calls it a prison farm versus just a straight prison; Garden = Farm and she shakes because she now knows she will die and being a lady she cannot sweat like a Man: Christ. *After all, if Aunty could be a lady at a time like this, so could I.*[136] Scout states. Of course, it is only a metaphorical death. Jem has already had his time in the Garden now it is up to Scout to understand her real purpose in the book. And to underscore this point, no longer will Atticus or Jem state that she does not understand something because she is not yet nine. Harper Lee could have used any age to signify understanding but purposefully uses nine to symbolize Christ's death as he dies in the ninth hour.

But it gets even better, how does Lee get in the kiss that condemns Christ? Brilliantly in my opinion. *...said Miss Maudie. "Are you together again, Jean Louise?" "Yes, ma'am." "Then let's join the ladies," she said grimly. "Calpurnia's on an errand for a few minutes, Grace," said Miss Maudie. "Let me pass you some more of those dewberry tarts, 'dyou hear what that cousin of mine did the other day, the one who likes to go fishing?..."*[137] The dewberry tarts represent the kiss of Judas, but here Lee does this with all women the opposite to the Gospel wherein all men are involved. Even the dewberries are in on the act as they are *dioecious* meaning that they are male and female, the tarts are female and eating them represents the kiss of death that Judas gives Christ. And, of course, many of the disciples were fishermen.

But Harper Lee's wry and ribald wit cannot be contained. Otherwise I could not have made the next Biblical connection. In the above scene Tom's death has been announced and he has been shot **17** times. And since Scout has seen the Enfield Prison Farm it has been **revealed** to her. And the only reason Lee adds that it was the size of a football field was to get in a veiled *Proverbs 25.2* reference to the number **22**, the number of men on a football field. So since she has seen the field and thus it has been **revealed** to her, we go the book of *Revelation* **and verse 22:17** does seem to have a relationship with Scout's shaking and a pretty damn good reason for Miss Maudie to tell her to stop it. *Revelation 22:17, The Spirit and the bride say "Come." And let everyone who hears say, "Come." And let everyone who is thirsty come. Let anyone who wishes take the water of life as a gift.* The word *come* is used three times and it had the same subtext and connotation in 1960 as it does now, Scout is shaking because she is "*cuming*", she is having an *orgasm*. But I could never even imagine Harper Lee stating this if asked by some affectionate fan, so silence will be her only recourse.

Scout's "death" is represented by her ham outfit in the pageant, that I have already designated as the Passion of the Christ. But there is a relationship that needs to be explored to understand why Scout is a ham versus a chicken, corn or cow as all would be part of the agricultural wonderland of

Maycomb County. This connection involves Saint Nicolas, our Santa Claus. According to legend, during a severe famine an evil butcher lured 3 children into his shop, killed them and was in the process of pickling them in order to sell them as cured ham. Saint Nick to the rescue, he sees right through the lies of the butcher and saves the children by making the sign of the cross. Scout is mocked and laughed at as she enters the stage as she misses her cue of **PORK**, spoken by Miss Merriweather. Christ is mocked in all four Gospels as He is being crucified.

There is no gospel of how Christ Resurrected and brought Himself back to life while in the tomb, but I think that Harper Lee is attempting to do just that as she describes Boo Radley. He will represent the Risen Christ, just as Scout is Christ on the Cross and Jem is the entombed Christ as he is drugged into unconsciousness after the attack. *When Boo Radley shuffled to his feet, light from the living room windows glistened on his forehead. Every move he made was uncertain, as if he were not sure his hands and feet could make proper contact with the things he touched.* (As they had recently been hammered through with nails this might be natural.) *He coughed his dreadful raling cough, and was so shaken he had to sit down again.* (Being pierced through to the heart and lungs will do that to a Guy.) *His hand searched for his hip pocket, and he pulled out a handkerchief. He coughed into it, then wiped his forehead.*[138] Thorns thrust into a it might require a forehead to be wiped. I believe that this fulfills John 20:7 (New

King James Version), *And the* **handkerchief** *that had been around His head, not lying with the other linen cloths, but folded together in a place by itself.* Scout even states it herself, *My small fantasy about him was alive again.*[139] Small fantasy being the opposite of the profound truth of the Resurrection is just more Ellen/Nelle opposite action.

And Lee gets in one last twist, one final surprise to finish the Biblical metaphors. She starts *TKAM* by stating in the first chapter that Alabama started at St. Stephen. St. Stephen is the first martyr and Saul/Paul is implicated in his death by holding the robes of the men stoning him to death. Hugo also includes the martyrdom of St. Stephen in *Part One, Book One, Chapter Eight of Les Misérables.* Heck Tate will represent Saul/Paul. He holds Scout's costume at the end and even though not blinded by the light like Paul the lights do come on in the most miraculous way. *Mr. Tate's boot hit the floorboards so hard the lights in Miss Maudie's bedroom went on. Miss Stephanie Crawford's lights went on.*[140] Tate declares that he is, *"…not a very good man…"*[141] In *Romans 8:18*, we read that Paul himself states, *For I know that nothing good dwells within me, that is, my flesh.* It is my personal opinion that Lee is trying to one up Hugo as he states of Jean Valjean, *The convict was transfigured into Christ.*[142] Hugo has no Saul/Paul character so Lee introduces him in *TKAM* but always with *Proverbs 25.2* in mind, **It is the glory of God to conceal things, but the glory of kings to search things out**.

So to sum it all up, this book as written is better than the book that you read, Lee would have had a tough time explaining it all if ever asked why Scout shakes or why the word *yawl* is only used 3 times or even why Hunt's *Light of the World* is the only picture in Calpurnia's church. Or why Atticus and Jean Valjean are two of the best shots in all of literature. Jean Valjean does not shoot small birds and of course, Atticus does not want mockingbirds killed. I hope that I have explained it all in a way that is understandable to all and that among other things, that the greatest story ever told is being retold in Harper Lee's fabulous book *To Kill a Mockingbird.*

BIBLIOGRAPHY

Bible passages from the *Catholic Youth Bible Revised*. New Revised Standard Version: Catholic Edition. Saint Mary's Press. The Scripture quotations contained herein are from the New Revised Standard Version Bible Catholic Edition copyright © 1993 and 1989 by the Division of Christian Education of the National Council of the Churches of Christ in the U.S.A. Used by permission. All rights reserved

Bulfinch, Thomas. *Bulfinch Illustrated Mythology*. Old Saybrook, CT. Konecky & Konecky.

Credit given to "The University of Alabama Libraries Special Collection" for the *Rammer Jammer* images

Flynt, Wayne. *Mockingbird Songs*. New York, N.Y. HarperCollins Publishers. 2017

Hugo, Victor. *Les Misérables*. New York, N.Y. The Modern Library. 2009

Lee, Harper. *To Kill a Mockingbird*. New York. N.Y. Grand Central Publishing. 1960.

Lee, Harper. *Go Set a Watchman*. New York. N.Y. HarperPerennial. ModernClassics. 2015

Mills, Marja. *The Mockingbird Next Door: Life With Harper Lee*. New York, N.Y. The Penguin Press. 2014

Shields, Charles. *Mockingbird*. New York, N.Y. St. Martin's Griffin. 2016

Shields, Charles, *I Am Scout*. New York, N.Y. Henry Holt and Company. 2008

ENDNOTES

1   Shields. *I Am Scout*, Page 97.
2   Shields. *I Am Scout*, page 6.
3   University of Alabama. *Rammer Jammer,* Volume 23 Number 2, November 1947 page 21.
4   Lee. *To Kill a Mockingbird,* page 212.
5   Lee. *To Kill a Mockingbird,* page 212.
6   Lee. *To Kill a Mockingbird,* page 213.
7   Lee. *To Kill a Mockingbird,* page 53.
8   Lee. *To Kill a Mockingbird,* page 97.
9   Flynt. *Mockingbird Songs,* page 64.
10   Mills. *The Mockingbird Next Door: Life With Harper Lee,* page 252.
11   Lee. *To Kill a Mockingbird,* page 372.
12   University of Alabama. *Rammer Jammer,* Volume 16 Number 3, November 1940 page 36 & Volume 21 Number 4, December 1945 page 25.
13   Lee. *To Kill a Mockingbird,* page 3.
14   University of Alabama. *Rammer Jammer,* Volume 25 Number 5, March 1950, page 15
15   Lee. *To Kill a Mockingbird,* page 16.
16   University of Alabama. *Rammer Jammer,* Volume 31 Number 6, April 1956 page 7.
17   Lee. *To Kill a Mockingbird,* page 16.
18   Lee. *To Kill a Mockingbird,* page 4.
19   University of Alabama. *Rammer Jammer,* Volume 25 Number 2, November 1949, page 13.
20   University of Alabama. *Rammer Jammer,* Volume 25 Number 2, November 1949, page 24.
21   Lee. *To Kill a Mockingbird,* page 51.

22 Lee. *To Kill a Mockingbird,* page 62.
23 University of Alabama. *Rammer Jammer,* Volume 25 Number 2, November 1949, page 12.
24 Lee. *To Kill a Mockingbird,* page 9.
25 University of Alabama. *Rammer Jammer,* Volume 25 Number 2, November 1949, page 21.
26 University of Alabama. *Rammer Jammer,* Volume 25 Number 2, November 1949, page 7.
27 Lee. *To Kill a Mockingbird,* page 14.
28 Lee. *To Kill a Mockingbird,* page 362.
29 Lee. *To Kill a Mockingbird,* page 61.
30 Lee. *To Kill a Mockingbird,* page 89.
31 University of Alabama. *Rammer Jammer,* Volume 25 Number 2, November 1949, page 21.
32 University of Alabama. *Rammer Jammer,* Volume 25 Number 2, November 1949, page 15.
33 Lee. *To Kill a Mockingbird,* page 258.
34 Hugo. *Les Misérables,* page *1189.*
35 Hugo. *Les Misérables,* page 1188.
36 Lee. *To Kill a Mockingbird,* page 119.
37 Lee. *To Kill a Mockingbird,* page 120.
38 Lee. *To Kill a Mockingbird,* page 120.
39 Lee. *To Kill a Mockingbird,* page 130.
40 Lee. *To Kill a Mockingbird,* page 127.
41 Lee. *To Kill a Mockingbird,* page 129-130.
42 University of Alabama. *Rammer Jammer,* Volume 8 Number 5, March 1932, page 11.
43 Lee. *To Kill a Mockingbird,* page 68.
44 Lee. *To Kill a Mockingbird,* page 85.
45 Lee. *To Kill a Mockingbird,* page 85.
46 Lee. *To Kill a Mockingbird,* page 85.
47 Lee. *To Kill a Mockingbird,* page 88.
48 Lee. *To Kill a Mockingbird,* page 92.
49 Lee. *To Kill a Mockingbird,* page 97.
50 Lee. *To Kill a Mockingbird,* page 98.
51 Lee. *To Kill a Mockingbird,* page 94.
52 Lee. *To Kill a Mockingbird,* page 148.
53 Lee. *To Kill a Mockingbird,* page 353

54 Lee. *To Kill a Mockingbird,* page 345
55 Lee. *To Kill a Mockingbird,* page 345
56 Lee. *To Kill a Mockingbird,* page 343.
57 Lee. *To Kill a Mockingbird,* page 339.
58 Lee. *To Kill a Mockingbird,* page 339.
59 Lee. *To Kill a Mockingbird,* page 339-340.
60 Lee. *To Kill a Mockingbird,* page 329.
61 Lee. *Go Set a Watchman,* page 110.
62 Lee. *To Kill a Mockingbird,* page 16.
63 Lee. *To Kill a Mockingbird,* page 48.
64 Lee. *To Kill a Mockingbird,* page 48.
65 Lee. *To Kill a Mockingbird,* page 22.
66 Lee. *To Kill a Mockingbird,* page 52.
67 Bulfinch. *Bulfinch Illustrated Mythology,* page 62.
68 Lee. *To Kill a Mockingbird,* page 158.
69 Lee. *To Kill a Mockingbird,* page 197.
70 Lee. *To Kill a Mockingbird,* page 204.
71 Lee. *To Kill a Mockingbird,* page 205.
72 Lee. *To Kill a Mockingbird,* page 205.
73 Lee. *To Kill a Mockingbird,* page 206
74 Lee. *To Kill a Mockingbird,* page 206-207.
75 Lee. *To Kill a Mockingbird,* page 200.
76 Lee. *To Kill a Mockingbird,* page 25.
77 Lee. *To Kill a Mockingbird,* page 28.
78 Lee. *To Kill a Mockingbird,* page 32.
79 Lee. *To Kill a Mockingbird,* page 33.
80 Lee. *To Kill a Mockingbird,* page 215.
81 Lee. *To Kill a Mockingbird,* page 267-268.
82 Lee. *To Kill a Mockingbird,* page 268-269
83 Lee. *To Kill a Mockingbird,* page 53.
84 Lee. *To Kill a Mockingbird,* page 56.
85 Lee. *Go Set a Watchman, page 61*
86 Lee. *To Kill a Mockingbird,* page 61.
87 Lee. *To Kill a Mockingbird,* page 67-68.
88 University of Alabama. *Rammer Jammer,* Volume 14 Number 1, October 1936, page 26.
89 University of Alabama. *Rammer Jammer,* Volume 4 Number 1, October 1927, cover page.

[90] Lee. *To Kill a Mockingbird*, page 101.

[91] Lee. *To Kill a Mockingbird*, page 102.

[92] Lee. *To Kill a Mockingbird*, page 102.

[93] Lee. *Go Set a Watchman*, page 107.

[94] Lee. *Go Set a Watchman*, page 107.

[95] Lee. *To Kill a Mockingbird*, page 112-113

[96] Lee. *To Kill a Mockingbird*, page 112

[97] Lee. *To Kill a Mockingbird*, page 112

[98] Hugo. *Les Misérables*, page 46.

[99] Lee. *To Kill a Mockingbird*, page 143.

[100] Lee. *To Kill a Mockingbird*, page 145.

[101] Lee. *To Kill a Mockingbird*, page 145.

[102] Lee. *To Kill a Mockingbird*, page 145.

[103] Lee. *To Kill a Mockingbird*, page 155.

[104] University of Alabama. *Rammer Jammer*, Volume 25 Number 2, November 1949, page 7.

[105] University of Alabama. *Rammer Jammer*, Volume 22 Number 4, December 1946, page 7.

[106] University of Alabama. *Rammer Jammer*, Volume 16 Number 6, March 1941, page 11.

[107] Lee. *To Kill a Mockingbird*, page 163.

[108] Lee. *To Kill a Mockingbird*, page 17.

[109] University of Alabama. *Rammer Jammer*, Volume 28 Number 3, December 1952, page 14.

[110] Lee. *To Kill a Mockingbird*, page 164.

[111] Lee. *To Kill a Mockingbird*, page 165.

[112] Lee. *To Kill a Mockingbird*, page 165.

[113] Lee. *To Kill a Mockingbird*, page 165.

[114] Lee. *To Kill a Mockingbird*, page 165.

[115] Lee. *To Kill a Mockingbird*, page 291.

[116] Hugo. *Les Misérables*, page 9.

[117] Hugo. *Les Misérables*, page 19.

[118] Lee. *To Kill a Mockingbird*, page 106.

[119] Hugo. *Les Misérables*, page 138.

[120] Lee. *To Kill a Mockingbird*, page 119.

[121] Hugo. *Les Misérables*, page 72.

[122] Lee. *To Kill a Mockingbird*, page 145.

[123] Hugo. *Les Misérables*, page 101.

[124] Hugo. *Les Misérables,* page 1189.
[125] Hugo. *Les Misérables,* page 1188.
[126] Hugo. *Les Misérables,* page 728.
[127] Lee. *To Kill a Mockingbird,* page 374.
[128] Hugo. *Les Misérables,* page 22.
[129] Lee. *To Kill a Mockingbird,* page 3-4.
[130] Hugo. *Les Misérables,* page 30.
[131] Lee. *To Kill a Mockingbird,* page 93.
[132] Hugo. *Les Misérables,* page 135.
[133] Lee. *To Kill a Mockingbird,* page 46.
[134] Hugo. *Les Misérables,* page 65.
[135] Lee. *To Kill a Mockingbird,* page 317.
[136] Lee. *To Kill a Mockingbird,* page 318.
[137] Lee. *To Kill a Mockingbird,* page 317.
[138] Lee. *To Kill a Mockingbird,* page 371.
[139] Lee. *To Kill a Mockingbird,* page 364,
[140] Lee. *To Kill a Mockingbird,* page 386.
[141] Lee. *To Kill a Mockingbird,* page 369.
[142] Hugo. *Les Misérables,* page 1186.